Party Food
for Vegetarians

Also by Linda Majzlik

Festive Food for Vegetarians (1991)

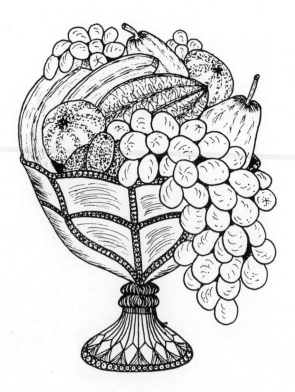

Party Food *for* Vegetarians

Recipes and illustrations by
Linda Majzlik

JON CARPENTER
Oxford

First published in 1995 by
Jon Carpenter, PO Box 129,
Oxford OX1 4PH

ISBN 1 897766 04 1

Designed and typeset by Sarah Tyzack,
Oxford

Printed and bound in England by
Biddles Ltd, Guildford and King's Lynn

CONTENTS

INTRODUCTION

THERE'S probably many a time that a vegetarian has been invited to a party and been disappointed to find that the only meat-free items included in the buffet were perhaps a slice of French bread and a salad. This has happened to me so often that I thought it was time to compile a cookery book of foods which all make suitable party fare for vegetarians.

Firstly, I hope this book will appeal to vegetarians who simply want some fresh ideas, or who might want to lay on a spread to impress their meat-eating friends. But secondly, I hope those meat-eating friends might also find it useful when inviting vegetarian friends to their parties! It will also help dispel the myth that vegetarians are a group of kill-joys who only eat bland and uninteresting foods.

As you will see, there is a vast assortment of tasty, attractive and satisfying foods that can easily be made without the use of meat. The recipes in this book range from tasty little party nibbles, dips and fondues, pastries and patés, salads and dressings, savoury biscuits and breads, chutneys and relishes, through to delicious cakes and desserts. There are ideas for sandwiches and fillings, as well as for garnishes to make your party platters look extra special. Even basic ingredients like rice, bread, eggs, pulses and cheese can be easily transformed into mouth-watering party fare.

Whether you are planning a cocktail party for ten or a buffet party for thirty or more guests, you will find recipes here to suit the occasion.

It's as well to plan your party as far ahead as possible, especially when catering for larger numbers. You will need this time for working out exactly what foods you are going to serve, and planning which ones can be made in advance and frozen. You may need to arrange to hire, or borrow from friends, items of cutlery, crockery, and glasses; to arrange also with friends or neighbours for the use of

1

fridge space nearer the time; and lastly to arrange to get together a willing band of helpers to help prepare the foods and set out the buffet table. There's nothing worse than when the host or hostess of the party spends most of the evening rushing backwards and forwards from the kitchen!

Lots of the food can be prepared in advance, then frozen until required. Some can be made the day before and refrigerated. Other dishes, such as salads and sandwiches, need to be prepared on the day to maintain freshness.

Plan to shop for non-perishables such as paper plates (if you use them), serviettes, tablecloths, cocktail sticks, doylies, tea, coffee and other drinks (soft and alcoholic) well in advance. This will prevent any last-minute panics and leave just the perishables to shop for prior to the party.

To save more time on the day of the party, it's a good idea – if possible – to lay the buffet table with tablecloths and arrange flowers or other decorations (depending on the type of party you are giving) on the day before. Plates, cutlery and serviettes for the guests to use can also be laid out and covered, leaving just the food to put out on the day just before the guests arrive. As some of your guests might be unfamiliar with vegetarian foods, you might like to make little labels for your party platters and dishes.

With a little forward planning it is possible to provide a veritable feast of entirely vegetarian, wholesome party fare which your guests will be sure to appreciate.

INGREDIENTS AND MEASURES

The following applies to the ingredients used in the recipes in this book.

AGAR AGAR A vegetable gelling and thickening powder which is a vegetarian/vegan alternative to gelatine.

CHEESES Most supermarkets and health food shops stock a whole range of vegetarian cheeses which are made with non-animal rennet.

CHESTNUTS Frozen chestnuts are by far the most convenient to use. They are ready-peeled and just need to be thawed before using. Dried chestnuts can also be used. These need to be soaked in water overnight, then rinsed and put in a fresh pan of water. Bring to the boil, cover, and simmer for 10 minutes. Drain, and then follow your chosen recipe. 6oz/175g of dried chestnuts will make about 8oz/225g when reconstituted.

EGGS All eggs are free range, size 3.

ESSENCES Available from health food shops, essences are natural flavourings as opposed to 'extracts' which are synthetic.

HERBS Unless otherwise stated, dried herbs are used in the recipes. If you are using fresh herbs, remember to double the quantity given.

MAYONNAISE SUBSTITUTE This egg-free soya-based alternative is available from health food shops. It is suitable for vegan use, as it contains no egg or dairy products.

MILK All milk is semi-skimmed.

PARMESAN CHEESE A soya-based Parmesan style seasoning is available from health food shops. It is suitable for vegan use as it contains no dairy products.

PEANUT BUTTER Unless otherwise stated, use the smooth variety.

SOY SAUCE Choose a brand that is naturally fermented without the use of chemicals. SHOYU is a light soy sauce, whilst TAMARI is dark and has a stronger flavour.

WORCESTER SAUCE Buy an equivalent from a health food shop, as most supermarket versions contain anchovies.

MEASURES

1 tablespoon = 15ml
1 dessertspoon = 10ml
1 teaspoon = 5ml
1 British pint = 20 fl.oz (in the recipes, pints refer to British pints)
1 American pint = 16 fl.oz
1 American measuring cup = 8 fl.oz

Note: use either imperial or metric measures: do not mix the two. All spoon measures are level unless otherwise stated.

GARNISHES

Give your platters of party foods a professional-looking finish with the addition of some attractive and edible garnishes. Lots of easily obtainable foods can be used to make garnishes which will add both colour and flavour, and will also enhance and complement your party dishes.

FRESH HERBS Parsley, mint, coriander, chives, dill and basil are all suitable, either as sprigs or finely chopped for sprinkling.

NUTS AND SEEDS Nuts can be used whole, chopped or flaked. They can be toasted to give extra flavour. Use sunflower, pumpkin, sesame and poppy seeds for sprinkling.

FRUITS Lemons, limes and oranges can be cut into thin wedge shapes or little triangles. To make triangles cut the fruits into slices ¼in/5mm thick, then cut each slice into 6 or 8 little triangle shapes. Make twists by cutting the fruits into thin slices and making a cut in each slice from the edge to about three-quarters through the slice. Shape each slice into a twist, either singly or use several slices to make a row. Finely grate the peel of citrus fruits and use for sprinkling, or use a citrus peeler for making peel curls. Apples, apricots, kiwi and star fruits can be cut into slices. Use seedless grapes, either whole or halved, and melon balls made with a ball cutter. Remember to sprinkle any fruits that might discolour with lemon juice.

VEGETABLES Cut raw vegetables such as carrot, courgette, celery, peppers, fennel, turnip and mooli into julienne (matchstick size) strips. Carrot, courgette, turnip and mooli can be grated or made into balls using a ball cutter. Cut different coloured peppers into little diamond shapes. Use button mushrooms whole or sliced – or make mushroom flowers: starting at the centre of the mushroom cap, make several cuts around the cap towards the edge, removing a small slice of mushroom each time. Thinly slice red and white onions and leeks and separate into rings. The leaves of celery and fennel also make attractive garnishes.

SALAD INGREDIENTS

Shredded lettuce Roll up lettuce leaves, then slice them thinly. Tomato lilies Use a sharp knife to make a series of zigzag cuts around the tomato through to the centre, until the two halves separate.

Tomato roses Peel a tomato with a sharp knife as if you were peeling an apple. This needs to be done in one piece. Curl the skin to give a rose effect.

Cherry tomatoes Use either whole or halved, or halved and stuffed with a savoury filling.

Radish flowers Cut petal-like shapes around the edge of the radish towards the centre. Soak in cold water for about an hour until they open out. Pat dry on kitchen paper before using.

Spring onion fans Cut spring onions into approximately 3in/8cm lengths. Finely slice the green part of the onions to about 1in/2½cm from the top. Soak in cold water for about 1 hour until they open out. Pat dry on kitchen paper before using.

Cucumber twists Cut some thin slices of cucumber. Make a cut in each of the slices from the edge to about three-quarters through the slice. Twist both sides in opposite directions.

Ridged cucumber slices Score the length of a cucumber with a fork or the point of a sharp knife, then cut into slices.

Cucumber butterflies Cut some slices of cucumber. Cut a triangle from opposite sides of each circle of cucumber to leave a butterfly shape.

Mustard and cress and *watercress* Trim and use in little bunches.

MISCELLANEOUS

Gherkin fans Make several length-ways cuts in each gherkin to within ¼in/5mm of the top. Spread out to make a fan effect.

Eggs Use hardboiled eggs either whole or chopped.

Olives Use stoned black or green olives either whole, halved or sliced.

Capers Finely chop and use for sprinkling.

Flavoured margarines See page 73. Pipe into little rosette shapes onto tomato and cucumber slices.

PARTY PLATTERS

TEMPT your guests with an exciting assortment of party foods presented imaginatively on large serving platters or plates. Pay special attention to arranging the foods, and include a variety of shapes, flavours and colours on each platter. With careful presentation and garnishing, you can achieve some very professional-looking results.

Included in this section is a selection of hot and cold foods, and advance preparation notes are given with each recipe.

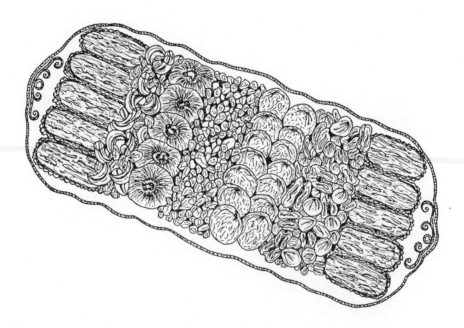

NOTE

The next three recipes – Pine kernel and mushroom medallions, Chestnut and walnut sausages, and Mixed nut balls – are all little fried savouries. All can either be made the day before required and refrigerated, or made in advance and frozen. They can all be served hot or cold. To serve hot, put them on an ovenproof plate, cover with foil and place in the oven at 170°C/ 325°F/Gas mark 3 for about 15 minutes – slightly longer if heating from frozen. They can be served just as they are arranged on a platter, or they can be put inside little wholemeal rolls or pitta breads with some mixed salad leaves and a thick dressing or relish.

Pine kernel and mushroom medallions

Makes 15

(See note above)

- 6oz/175g mushrooms, wiped and finely chopped
- 4oz/100g pine kernels
- 1 onion, peeled and grated
- 2oz/50g fresh wholemeal breadcrumbs
- 1oz/25g wholemeal flour
- 1 egg, beaten
- 1 teaspoon thyme
- 1 teaspoon parsley
- black pepper
- extra flour
- sunflower oil

Put the pine kernels in a greaseproof bag and roll with a rolling pin until crushed. Transfer the crushed pine kernels to a mixing bowl and add the mushrooms, onion, breadcrumbs, 1oz/25g flour, thyme and parsley. Season with black pepper and stir well. Add the egg and mix thoroughly until the mixture binds together. Take rounded dessertspoonfuls of the mixture and shape into balls.

Put some flour in a shallow bowl and roll each ball in flour until coated. Flatten each ball into a round approximately ½in/1cm thick. Transfer the rounds to a plate, cover and refrigerate for a couple of hours.

Shallow fry the medallions in hot sunflower oil for a few minutes each side until golden brown. Drain on kitchen paper and serve hot or cold.

Chestnut and walnut sausages

Makes 16

(See note above)

- 4oz/100g shelled chestnuts, grated
- 2oz/50g walnuts, finely grated
- 2oz/50g fresh wholemeal breadcrumbs
- 1oz/25g wholemeal flour
- 1 small onion, peeled and grated
- 1 egg, beaten ➋

1 dessertspoon Worcester sauce
1 dessertspoon sherry
1 rounded teaspoon parsley
1 rounded teaspoon mixed herbs
½ teaspoon paprika
black pepper
wheatgerm
sunflower oil

Put all the ingredients, except the wheatgerm and sunflower oil, in a mixing bowl. Mix thoroughly until the mixture binds together. Take rounded dessertspoonfuls of the mixture and shape into small sausages about 2in/5cm long. Roll the sausages in wheatgerm until completely covered. Transfer them to a plate, cover and chill for a couple of hours.

Shallow fry in hot sunflower oil until golden. Drain on kitchen paper and serve hot or cold.

Mixed nut balls

Makes 15

(See note on page 7)

4oz/100g mixed nuts, grated
4oz/100g carrot, scraped and grated
2oz/50g fresh wholemeal bread-crumbs
1oz/25g wheatgerm
1 onion, peeled and grated
1 rounded tablespoon peanut butter
1 egg, beaten

1 teaspoon soy sauce
1 rounded teaspoon mixed herbs
black pepper
1oz/25g ground almonds
sunflower oil

Put the ground almonds in a shallow bowl and set aside. Place the remaining ingredients, except the sunflower oil, in a mixing bowl and mix thoroughly. Take dessert-spoonfuls of the mixture and shape into balls. Roll the balls in the ground almonds until completely covered, put them on a plate, cover and chill for a couple of hours.

Shallow fry the balls in hot sunflower oil until golden. Drain on kitchen paper and serve either hot or cold.

Peanut and raisin stuffed dates

Makes 36

Can be made the day before required and refrigerated.

36 boxed dessert dates
2oz/50g shelled peanuts, finely chopped
2oz/50g raisins, finely chopped
1 tablespoon peanut butter
4 rounded tablespoons quark

Slit the dates and remove the stones. Mix the peanuts with the raisins, peanut butter and quark until well combined. Open the dates and fill each with some of the mixture. Arrange on a serving plate. Cover and chill.

Chick pea and peanut rolls

Makes 20

These can be prepared the day before required and refrigerated. The rolls are best shaped and rolled in the coating a few hours before serving, and then refrigerated again.

- 8oz/225g cooked chick peas, grated
- 8oz/225g cottage cheese, mashed
- 2oz/50g shelled peanuts, ground
- 8 spring onions, trimmed and finely chopped
- 2 rounded tablespoons peanut butter
- ½ teaspoon paprika
- 2 teaspoons chives
- 1 teaspoon soy sauce
- black pepper
- 5oz/150g shelled peanuts, finely chopped

Put the finely chopped peanuts in a bowl and set aside. Put the remaining ingredients in a mixing bowl and mix thoroughly. Take heaped teaspoonfuls of the mixture and shape into little rolls. Roll each shape in the chopped peanuts until completely coated. Arrange the rolls on a serving plate. Cover and refrigerate for a couple of hours.

Almond and oat buttons

Makes 24

These can be prepared the day before required and refrigerated. They are best shaped and rolled in the coating a few hours before serving, and then refrigerated again.

- 4oz/100g flaked almonds, finely chopped
- 4oz/100g low-fat curd cheese
- 2oz/50g Scottish oatcake biscuits, crushed
- 2 rounded tablespoons almond butter
- 2 teaspoons chives
- ½ teaspoon yeast extract
- black pepper

Put the curd cheese, almond butter, yeast extract and chives in a mixing bowl. Season with black pepper and mix until well combined. Work in the flaked almonds. Take rounded teaspoonfuls of the mixture and roll each into a ball. Flatten each ball slightly into a round shape. Roll each round in the crushed biscuits until covered all over. Transfer to a serving plate. Cover and chill for a couple of hours.

Watercress and Stilton balls

Makes 24

These can be prepared the day before required and refrigerated. They are best shaped and rolled in

9

the coating a few hours before serving, and then again refrigerated.

  1 bunch of watercress, finely chopped
  ½ bunch of watercress, trimmed
  8oz/225g blue Stilton, mashed
  4oz/100g rye bread, made into crumbs
  3oz/75g quark
  1 teaspoon chervil
  black pepper

Put the finely chopped watercress, Stilton, quark and chervil in a mixing bowl. Season with black pepper and mix thoroughly until the mixture binds together. Put the rye breadcrumbs in a bowl. Take heaped teaspoonfuls of the mixture and shape into small balls. Roll each ball in the breadcrumbs until coated all over. Arrange the trimmed watercress round the edge of a serving plate and place the balls in the centre.

Cover and chill for a couple of hours.

Sunflower and raisin bites

Makes 24

These can be prepared the day before required and refrigerated. They are best shaped and rolled in the coating a few hours before serving, and then refrigerated again.

  8oz/225g cottage cheese
  4oz/100g raisins, chopped
  2oz/50g fresh wholemeal bread-crumbs
  2 rounded tablespoons sunflower spread
  4oz/100g sunflower seeds
  fresh parsley sprigs

Put the cottage cheese, raisins, sunflower spread and breadcrumbs in a bowl and mix until combined. Take heaped teaspoonfuls of the mixture and roll into balls. Put the sunflower seeds in a bowl and roll each ball in the seeds until coated all over. Refrigerate for a few hours. Serve garnished with the fresh parsley.

Edam and walnut toasties

Makes 16

The toppings can be prepared several hours in advance. The bread can be cut, spread with margarine and refrigerated. This leaves just the putting together and baking before your guests arrive.

  4 thick slices wholemeal bread
  2oz/50g Edam cheese, grated
  1oz/25g walnuts, grated
  2 rounded tablespoons fromage frais
  1 tablespoon white wine
  black pepper
  1 teaspoon chives
  sunflower margarine

Spread one side of each slice of bread lightly with sunflower margarine. Mix the Edam with the walnuts, fromage frais, wine and chives. Season with black pepper and mix thoroughly. Spread this mixture evenly onto the plain sides of the bread. Cut each slice of bread into four triangles and place with the margarine side down on a baking sheet. Bake in a preheated oven at 190°C/375°F/Gas mark 5 for about 15 minutes until golden. Transfer to a serving plate and serve hot.

....

Mini pizza toasts

Makes 24

The toppings can be prepared several hours in advance. The bread can be cut, spread with margarine and refrigerated. This leaves just the putting together and baking before your guests arrive.

  1 wholemeal French stick
  sunflower margarine
  8oz/225g tomatoes, skinned and
    chopped
  4oz/100g mushrooms, wiped and
    finely chopped
  2oz/50g green pepper, finely
    chopped
  2oz/50g red pepper, finely
    chopped
  1 small onion or shallot, peeled
    and finely chopped
  2 garlic cloves, crushed
  1 tablespoon olive oil
  1 tablespoon tomato purée

  black pepper
  2 teaspoons oregano
  2oz/50g Cheddar cheese, grated
  chives

Cut the French stick into 24 round slices about ¾in/2cm thick. Spread both sides of each slice lightly with sunflower margarine. Lay the slices on a baking sheet and bake in a preheated oven at 180°C/350°F/Gas mark 4 for 5 minutes.

Heat the oil and gently fry the onion, garlic and peppers until softened. Add the mushrooms and fry for 2 minutes. Add the tomatoes, tomato purée and oregano and season with black pepper. Stir well and cook for a further 5 minutes. Spoon the hot mixture evenly onto the French bread slices. Spread the grated cheese on top and sprinkle with chives. Return to the oven for 5 minutes until the cheese melts. Serve hot.

....

Mushroom and cashew nut croustades

If you want to serve these little croustades hot, make the filling several hours in advance, then cover and refrigerate. Likewise line the tart tins with the bread and refrigerate, leaving just the putting together and baking until before your guests arrive. If you want to serve them cold, they can be made the day before required and refrigerated. ➥

11

4 large, medium-thick slices
  wholemeal bread

4oz/100g mushrooms, wiped and
  finely chopped

2oz/50g cashew nuts

2oz/50g cottage cheese, mashed

1 garlic clove, crushed

1 teaspoon olive oil

½ teaspoon thyme

½ teaspoon parsley

black pepper

dash of soy sauce

sunflower margarine

Roll each slice of bread with a rolling pin to flatten slightly. Cut each slice into four 2¼in/5½cm diameter circles using a pastry cutter. Lightly spread one side of each of the circles with margarine. Press the circles into tart tins, margarine side down.

Heat the oil and gently fry the garlic, add the mushrooms, and fry for 1 minute while stirring. Strain the juice from the mushrooms and discard. Put the mushrooms in a mixing bowl. Reserve 16 cashew nut halves and grate the rest. Put the grated cashews in a shallow baking tin and place under a hot grill until golden. Add them to the mixing bowl together with the cottage cheese, thyme, parsley and soy sauce. Season with black pepper and mix thoroughly.

Divide the mixture between the 16 bread bases and spread out evenly. Press a cashew nut half on top of

each croustade and bake in a preheated oven at 180°C/350°F/ Gas mark 4 for 20–25 minutes until golden. Serve hot or cold.

....

Onion and pepper cheesecakes

Makes 12

These can be made the day before required and refrigerated, or made in advance and frozen. If frozen, thaw at room temperature for about 3 hours before serving.

BASES

2oz/50g porridge oats

2oz/50g medium oatmeal

1oz/25g fresh wholemeal bread-
  crumbs

1oz/25g Cheddar cheese, grated

1oz/25g sunflower margarine

1 tablespoon grated Parmesan
  cheese

1 teaspoon chives

2 tablespoons milk

FILLING

8oz/225g onion, peeled and finely
  chopped

8oz/225g mixed peppers (i.e. red,
  yellow, green, orange), finely
  chopped

6oz/175g low-fat curd cheese

1oz/25g Cheddar cheese, grated

1 egg, beaten

1 garlic clove, crushed

1 tablespoon olive oil

1 teaspoon parsley

½ teaspoon thyme
¼ teaspoon mustard powder
black pepper

First make the bases. Melt the margarine over a low heat. Remove from the heat and stir in the porridge oats, oatmeal, bread-crumbs, Cheddar, Parmesan and chives. Add the milk and mix thoroughly. Divide the mixture between the holes of a 12-hole base-lined and greased muffin tin. Press the mixture down firmly with the back of the spoon until flat. Cover and refrigerate whilst making the filling.

Heat the oil and gently fry the onion, peppers and garlic for 10 minutes. Remove from the heat and add the rest of the filling ingredients. Mix well, then spoon the filling evenly over the bases. Bake in a preheated oven at 180°C/ 350°F/Gas mark 4 for 35–40 minutes until golden and set.

Allow to cool slightly in the tin, then run a sharp knife round the edges to loosen. Carefully remove from the tin and peel off the base linings. Refrigerate for a few hours until cold.

Spinach and courgette cheesecakes

Makes 12

These can be made the day before required and refrigerated, or made in advance and frozen. If frozen, thaw at room temperature for about 3 hours before serving.

BASES

As for Onion and pepper cheese-cakes (see previous recipe).

FILLING

6oz/175g frozen chopped spinach, thawed

6oz/175g courgette, grated

4oz/100g low-fat curd cheese

4oz/100g dolcelatte cheese, finely chopped or crumbled

1 egg, beaten

1 small onion, peeled and finely chopped

1 dessertspoon olive oil

1 teaspoon marjoram

1/8 teaspoon ground bay leaves

black pepper

Make up the bases exactly as for Onion and pepper cheesecakes.

Heat the oil and gently fry the onion until softened. Put the spinach in a fine sieve and press out excess water using the back of a spoon. Remove the onion from the heat and add the spinach and remaining filling ingredients. Mix thoroughly, then spoon the filling evenly over the bases. Bake in a

13

preheated oven at 180°C/350°F/
Gas mark 4 for 35–40 minutes until
golden and set.

Allow to cool slightly in the tin,
then run a sharp knife round the
edges to loosen. Carefully remove
from the tin and peel off the base
linings. Refrigerate for a few hours
until cold.

....

Scotch eggs

Makes 8

Can be made the day before
required, and refrigerated.

 8 hardboiled eggs, shelled
 8oz/225g mixed nuts, ground
 8oz/225g fresh wholemeal bread-
   crumbs
 4 rounded dessertspoons cashew
   nut butter
 4 eggs, beaten
 2 tablespoons milk
 4 teaspoons chives
 4 teaspoons mixed herbs
 2 teaspoons soy sauce
 1 teaspoon paprika
 black pepper
 sunflower oil
 fresh parsley sprigs

Put the ground nuts, breadcrumbs,
chives, mixed herbs and paprika in
a mixing bowl. Season with black
pepper and add the cashew nut
butter. Rub in until well combined.
Add the beaten eggs, milk and soy
sauce and mix thoroughly.

Divide the mixture into 8 equal
portions. Carefully mould one
portion of mixture around each of
the hardboiled eggs until they are
completely covered. Deep fry in
hot sunflower oil for a few minutes
until golden. Drain on kitchen
paper and allow to cool, then
refrigerate until cold.

Carefully cut each Scotch egg in
half and arrange them on a serving
plate. Garnish with fresh parsley
sprigs to serve.

....

Tortilla wedges

Serves 8/10

Can be made the day before
required, and refrigerated.

 4 eggs
 8oz/225g potatoes, peeled and
   sliced
 2oz/50g cooked red kidney beans
 2oz/50g button mushrooms,
   wiped and sliced
 2oz/50g frozen sweetcorn kernels
 2oz/50g frozen peas
 2oz/50g red pepper, finely
   chopped
 2oz/50g frozen cooked chopped
   spinach, thawed
 1oz/25g Cheddar cheese, grated
 1 small onion, peeled and finely
   chopped
 2 garlic cloves, crushed
 2 dessertspoons olive oil
 1 teaspoon thyme
 1 teaspoon oregano

black pepper
tomato wedges
chopped fresh chives

Cook the potato slices until just tender, then drain and chop roughly. Cook the sweetcorn and peas, drain and set aside. Heat 1 dessertspoon of olive oil in a 10in/25cm non-stick frying pan and fry the onion, garlic and red pepper for 10 minutes. Add the other dessertspoon of oil, together with the potatoes and mushrooms, and fry for 1 minute.

Beat the eggs with the spinach, cheese, thyme and oregano and season with black pepper. Add to the pan together with the sweet-corn, peas and kidney beans. Cook the tortilla for about 10 minutes without stirring until the egg sets on the top. Remove the pan from the heat and place it under a hot grill for about 5 minutes until golden and set. Carefully slide the tortilla onto a plate and allow to cool, then refrigerate until cold. Cut into wedges and serve garnished with tomato wedges and chopped chives.

Courgette and carrot roulade

Serves 12

Can be made the day before required, and refrigerated.

8oz/225g courgettes, grated
3 eggs, separated
½oz/15g sunflower margarine
½oz/15g fine wholemeal self-raising flour
1 rounded teaspoon parsley
1 rounded teaspoon thyme
black pepper
12oz/350g carrots, scraped and chopped
2oz/50g smoked Cheddar cheese, grated
1 teaspoon caraway seeds

Steam the carrots until tender, then mash. Season with black pepper and add the caraway seeds. Allow to cool, then refrigerate until cold.

Melt the margarine over a low heat, add the flour and stir for 30 seconds. Transfer to a mixing bowl and add the courgettes, beaten egg yolks, parsley and thyme. Season with black pepper and mix well. Whisk the egg whites until stiff and fold into the courgette mixture. Line a 13x9in/33x23cm Swiss roll tin with greaseproof paper and grease. Spoon the courgette mixture into the tin and spread out evenly to cover the base of the tin completely.

Bake in a preheated oven at 180°C/350°F/Gas mark 4 for about 30 minutes until golden.

Slide a sharp knife around the edges to loosen and turn out onto a wire rack. Carefully remove the greaseproof paper. Place a clean

15

sheet of greaseproof paper on the roulade and roll up loosely, starting from one of the long sides. Allow to cool.

Mix the grated cheese with the carrot. Unroll the roulade and remove the greaseproof paper. Spread the carrot mixture evenly over the roulade, making sure it goes right up to the edges. Roll up again, starting at one of the long sides, and transfer to a large plate or tin with the join underneath.

Cover and chill for a couple of hours. Cut into 12 equal slices and arrange on a serving plate.

....

Tacos filled with Mexican salad

To prepare in advance, mix all the salad ingredients together except for the avocado. This can be done the day before and refrigerated. Add the avocado up to 2 hours before serving, but do not fill the tacos with salad until the last moment to prevent them from softening.

12 taco shells
1lb/450g firm ripe tomatoes, chopped
8oz/225g cooked red kidney beans
4oz/100g frozen sweetcorn kernels
8 spring onions, trimmed and finely sliced
2 just ripe avocado pears, peeled, stoned and diced

2 garlic cloves, crushed
2 teaspoons olive oil
1 teaspoon Worcester sauce
2 tablespoons lemon juice
dash of tabasco sauce
1/4 teaspoon chilli powder
black pepper
2 teaspoons marjoram
2 teaspoons oregano
shredded crisp lettuce leaves

Cook the sweetcorn, drain, and rinse under cold running water. Drain well and put in a mixing bowl with the tomatoes, kidney beans, spring onions, avocado and garlic. Add the chilli powder, marjoram and oregano and season with black pepper. Mix the olive oil with the Worcester sauce, lemon juice and tabasco sauce. Pour over the salad and toss thoroughly. Put a little shredded lettuce into each taco shell and fill with the salad mixture.

....

Sunflower tomato lilies

Makes 12

Use firm, just ripe tomatoes for this recipe. The lilies can be made the day before and refrigerated.

6 medium-sized tomatoes
4oz/100g cottage cheese, mashed
4 spring onions, trimmed and finely chopped
1 tablespoon sunflower spread
1 teaspoon soy sauce

1 teaspoon chives
black pepper
sunflower seeds
fresh parsley

Cut the tomatoes in half in a zigzag pattern to make 12 lilies. Remove the insides of the tomatoes and turn the shells upside down to drain. Chop the tomato flesh and put it in a sieve to drain off the juice. Put the chopped tomato in a mixing bowl with the cottage cheese, spring onions, sunflower spread, soy sauce and chives and season with black pepper. Mix thoroughly.

Dry the tomato shells on kitchen paper. Divide the filling between the 12 shells and sprinkle sunflower seeds on top. Transfer to a serving plate and garnish with fresh parsley. Cover and chill before serving.

....

Stuffed baked mushrooms

Makes 30

If you want to serve these stuffed mushrooms cold, make them on the morning of your celebration and refrigerate.

To serve hot, prepare them up to the baking stage, then cover and refrigerate. Pop them in the oven just before your guests arrive.

30 medium-sized mushrooms
1 small onion, peeled and grated
2 garlic cloves, crushed
2oz/50g red pepper, finely chopped
2oz/50g green pepper, finely chopped
2oz/50g walnuts, grated
2oz/50g fresh wholemeal bread-crumbs
2oz/50g Gruyère cheese, grated
2 tablespoons sherry
1 tablespoon olive oil
2 teaspoons thyme
2 teaspoons chervil
black pepper
extra olive oil
fresh parsley

Wipe the mushrooms and remove and chop the stalks. Heat the tablespoon of oil and gently fry the onion, garlic, red and green peppers and chopped mushroom stalks for 10 minutes. Remove from the heat and add the walnuts, breadcrumbs, Gruyère, sherry, thyme and chervil and season with black pepper. Mix well.

Lightly brush the outsides of the mushrooms with olive oil and fill each mushroom with some of the filling. Place the filled mushrooms in a casserole dish and bake in a preheated oven at 180°C/350°F/Gas mark 4 for 20 minutes.

Transfer to a serving plate and garnish with fresh parsley. Serve hot or cold.

Stuffed vine leaves

Makes 32

These can be prepared the day before and refrigerated. Serve them with a yoghurt-based dip or dressing: see Dips (page 52) and Dressings (page 92).

32 vine leaves

4oz/100g bulgar wheat

10 fl.oz/300ml boiling water

½ teaspoon yeast extract

1 dessertspoon soy sauce

1 tablespoon sunflower oil

1 onion, peeled and finely chopped

2 garlic cloves, crushed

4oz/100g dried dates, finely chopped

2oz/50g sultanas

1oz/25g pine kernels, chopped

1oz/25g walnuts, chopped

2 teaspoons coriander seeds, crushed

½ teaspoon ground cinnamon

¼ teaspoon cayenne pepper

black pepper

5 fl.oz/150ml water

2 fl.oz/50ml olive oil

1 fl.oz/25ml lemon juice

lemon wedges

Wash the vine leaves thoroughly, then put them in a large bowl of boiling water. Leave to stand for 20 minutes, rinse and drain. Dissolve the yeast extract and soy sauce in the 10 fl.oz/300ml boiling water. Add the bulgar wheat and leave to stand for 15 minutes. Heat the sunflower oil and gently fry the onion and garlic until softened. Remove from the heat and add the soaked bulgar wheat, dates, sultanas, pine kernels, walnuts, coriander seeds, cinnamon and cayenne pepper. Season with black pepper and mix thoroughly.

Take a vine leaf and place it shiny side down. Place a dessertspoon of the filling mixture in the centre. Fold in the sides of the leaf, then roll up to enclose the filling. Repeat with the other vine leaves. Pack the stuffed vine leaves with the seams underneath in a lightly oiled casserole dish. Mix the olive oil with the water and lemon juice and pour over the stuffed vine leaves. Cover tightly with foil and bake in a preheated oven at 180°C/350°F/Gas mark 4 for 45 minutes.

Transfer to a serving plate and allow to cool, then refrigerate until cold. Garnish with lemon wedges.

Stuffed avocado pears

Serves 8

To prevent the avocado from discolouring, avoid cutting and mashing the flesh more than 2 hours before serving. The rest of the filling ingredients can be mixed together and refrigerated the day before, leaving just the mashed avocado to add before serving.

4 ripe avocado pears

12oz/350g cooked chick peas, grated

4oz/100g Edam cheese, grated

black pepper

1 tablespoon chives

1 tablespoon lemon juice

paprika

Cut the avocado pears in half and remove the stones. Scoop out the avocado flesh and reserve the shells. Mash the flesh with the lemon juice and put in a mixing bowl with the chick peas, Edam and chives. Season with black pepper and mix thoroughly. Divide the mixture between the 8 avocado shells. Fork over the filling to neaten and sprinkle the tops with paprika to serve.

....

Buckwheat crêpes with creamy spinach filling

Makes 20

The pancakes can be made several hours before required and refrigerated. They are best filled just before serving.

BATTER

2oz/50g plain wholemeal flour

2oz/50g buckwheat flour

1 egg

10 fl.oz/300ml milk

black pepper

sunflower oil

FILLING

8oz/225g cottage cheese

8oz/225g frozen cooked chopped spinach, thawed

4 spring onions, trimmed and finely chopped

black pepper

½ teaspoon grated nutmeg

1 teaspoon marjoram

Whisk the egg with the milk and add the wholemeal and buckwheat flours. Season with black pepper and beat until smooth. Cover and leave to stand for 1 hour.

Brush a large non-stick frying pan with sunflower oil. Heat until hot, then use 1 tablespoonful of batter to make a pancake measuring about 3½–4in/9–10cm diameter. About 3 pancakes can be made at a time in a 10in/25cm frying pan. Allow the pancakes to cool, then refrigerate till cold.

Put the spinach in a fine sieve and press out excess water using the back of a spoon. Transfer the spinach to a mixing bowl and add the remaining filling ingredients. Mix thoroughly. Lay the cold pancakes on a flat surface and divide the filling between them. Roll the pancakes up to enclose the filling and secure with cocktail sticks to prevent them from opening up.

Stuffed pepper slices

Serves 10–12

Slices of pepper with a savoury filling might look very fiddly to make, but they are in fact very easy to prepare.

> 4 peppers (1 red, 1 green, 1 orange, 1 yellow), each weighing about 5oz/150g
> fresh parsley

Wash the peppers and dry them on kitchen paper. Cut the stalks from the peppers, leaving just a small hole at the top of each pepper through which to put the filling. Carefully remove the membranes and pips through the holes.

Prepare the 4 fillings (see below). Use a teaspoon to spoon a different filling into each pepper. After each teaspoonful, press down firmly with the back of the spoon. Continue until each pepper is full. Cover the filled peppers with cling film and refrigerate for a few hours or overnight.

Using a sharp knife, cut each pepper into slices each about ³⁄₈in/9mm thick. Neaten the filling if necessary and arrange the slices on a serving plate. Garnish with fresh parsley to serve.

Cashew nut and cottage cheese filling

> 2oz/50g cashew nuts, finely chopped
> 3oz/75g cottage cheese, mashed
> ½ teaspoon thyme
> ½ teaspoon parsley
> black pepper

Put the chopped cashew nuts on an ovenproof tray and place under a hot grill until golden. Allow to cool, then mix thoroughly with the remaining ingredients.

Peanut and raisin filling

> 3oz/75g shelled peanuts, ground
> 1oz/25g raisins, finely chopped
> 1 rounded tablespoon peanut butter
> 1 rounded tablespoon quark
> black pepper

Mix all the ingredients thoroughly.

Smoked cheese and carrot filling

> 2oz/50g smoked Cheddar cheese, grated
> 2oz/50g carrot, scraped and grated
> 1oz/25g ricotta cheese
> ¼ teaspoon caraway seeds
> 1 teaspoon chives
> black pepper

Mix all the ingredients thoroughly.

Cheesy chick pea and sunflower filling

2oz/50g cooked chick peas, grated
1oz/25g Cheddar cheese, grated
1oz/25g sunflower seeds, chopped
1 rounded tablespoon tahini
1 tablespoon milk
1 rounded teaspoon chives
1 teaspoon soy sauce
black pepper

Mix all the ingredients thoroughly.

Dried fruit and nut platter

Prepare an exotic looking platter made from a variety of dried fruits and nuts. Choose from no-soak ready-to-eat apricots and figs, boxed stoned dates, pineapple and paw paw chunks, banana chips, raisins, pistachios, Brazils, pecans, cashews, hazel nuts, almonds and macadamias, or whatever else takes your fancy! Not only health food shops but now also most supermarkets stock a vast range of dried fruits and nuts.

Arrange the fruits and nuts in rows on a long oblong plate or platter, or alternatively on a divided serving plate. Allow about 2oz/50g of mixed fruits and nuts per person.

The platter can be prepared the day before required, covered tightly with cling film and left in a cool place.

Mixed cheese platter

With more and more vegetarian versions of traditional cheeses appearing in the shops, it is now possible to prepare a really interesting platter comprising a variety of cheeses.

Allow about 2oz/50g of cheese per person.

As well as the English Cheddars, look out for vegetarian goat's cheese, blue cheeses, soft cheeses and continental cheeses. Choose a selection of cheeses to complement one another in taste and colour. Cut them into bite-size portions and arrange them attractively on a serving platter with bite-size chunks of celery and mixed peppers, cherry tomatoes and seedless grapes. Soft cheeses can be mixed with chopped nuts and herbs, then shaped into balls or logs and rolled in finely chopped fresh herbs.

The platter can be prepared several hours before required, covered with cling film and refrigerated.

Most cheeses are best served at room temperature, so remove the platter from the fridge about an hour before serving. Garnish the platter with fresh herbs. Allow about 2oz/50g of cheese per person and serve with a selection of savoury biscuits and breads and chutneys.

Some quick ideas

Thread cubes or balls of different cheeses with cubes of pineapple, seedless grapes, cherry tomatoes, stoned olives, melon balls, small chunks of celery and peppers onto 6in/15cm cocktail sticks to make cheese salad kebabs.

Hardboil some eggs. Cut in half lengthwise, remove the yolks and mash them. Mix with some curd cheese, mayonnaise and curry paste to taste. Pipe the mixture into the hollowed-out whites.

Pipe one of the sandwich spreads (see page74) onto some small savoury crackers. Garnish with fresh herbs and chopped olives.

Make 4 straight slits in some firm small tomatoes to within ¼in/5mm of their bases. Put a thin slice of mozzarella cheese and some sliced olives in each slit. Garnish with fresh basil leaves.

Cut celery sticks into 4in/10cm lengths. Pipe one of the sandwich spreads (see page 74) into the hollows. Likewise slice the tops off some cherry tomatoes. Carefully scoop out the centres and fill with a sandwich spread. Mushrooms can be wiped and filled in the same way.

Cut some grapefruits or oranges in half. Take out the segments using a serrated knife and reserve the shells. Remove the membrane from the segments and discard. Chop the flesh and mix with salad ingredients of your choice. Pile the salad into the shells and top with a thick dressing.

Drain some tinned apricot halves and dry them on kitchen paper. Mash some blue cheese with fromage frais until a thick piping consistency is achieved. Pipe the mixture into the hollows of the apricots.

PASTRIES

WHEN it comes to making pastries for a party, you can really start to plan in advance. Unless otherwise stated in the recipe, most of the pastries in this section can be made up to 4 weeks before required and frozen.

To serve the pastries cold, simply thaw at room temperature for a few hours before serving. If you want to serve your pastries warm, spread them out frozen on a baking sheet, cover with foil and put in a moderate oven for 20–30 minutes until heated thoroughly.

It's always a good idea to make more pastries than you think you will need. Then, if more guests than anticipated arrive or the food starts to run low, you can easily warm some more in the oven.

Choose a variety of different types of pastries in various shapes and sizes and present them on large serving platters or tiered cake stands.

Chestnut and vegetable plait

Serves 10

8oz/225g puff pastry
8oz/225g shelled chestnuts, grated
6oz/175g carrots, scraped and grated
6oz/175g courgette, grated
1 onion, peeled and grated
1 egg, beaten
1 tablespoon vegetable oil
1 dessertspoon soy sauce
1 rounded teaspoon parsley
1 rounded teaspoon thyme
½ teaspoon paprika
black pepper
milk
poppy seeds

Heat the oil and gently fry the onion and chestnuts for a couple of minutes whilst stirring. Remove from the heat and add the carrot, courgette, soy sauce, parsley, thyme, paprika and egg. Season with black pepper and mix thoroughly. Roll out the pastry on a floured board to an oblong shape measuring 16x10in/40x25cm. Transfer to a large greased baking sheet.

Spread the filling lengthwise down the middle 4in/10cm of the pastry. Cut horizontal strips ¾in/2cm wide to within ½in/1cm of the filling down each side of the pastry. Lift alternate strips of pastry over the filling to enclose completely and give a plaited effect. Brush with milk and sprinkle with poppy seeds. Bake in a preheated oven at 170°C/325°F/Gas mark 3 for about 35 minutes until golden. Cut into 10 equal portions and serve warm or cold.

Peanut and lentil paté en croûte

Makes 16

PASTRY
9oz/250g fine wholemeal self-raising flour
3½oz/90g sunflower margarine
1 rounded tablespoon peanut butter
milk

FILLING
4oz/100g brown lentils
4oz/100g cottage cheese, mashed
2oz/50g shelled peanuts, ground
1oz/25g raisins, chopped
1 onion, peeled and finely chopped
1 egg, beaten
3 tablespoons milk
1 dessertspoon sunflower oil
1 dessertspoon soy sauce
1 rounded teaspoon parsley
¼ teaspoon cayenne pepper
black pepper

Soak the lentils for a few hours, then rinse and put in a large pan of water. Bring to the boil, cover and simmer briskly for about 40 minutes until tender. Drain and set aside. Heat the oil and gently fry the onion until softened. Remove from the heat and add the cooked lentils and the remaining filling ingredients. Mix thoroughly and set aside.

Rub the margarine and peanut butter into the flour, then add enough milk to bind. Turn out onto a floured board and knead.

Cut the dough in half and roll out one piece to line the base of a greased 12x6in/32x16cm baking tin. Spread the filling evenly over the pastry base. Roll out the other piece of dough to the same size and place on top of the filling. Press down lightly.

Score the top of the pastry in a zigzag pattern with a sharp knife. Cut through into sixteen 3x1½in/ 8x4cm fingers. Brush the tops with milk and bake in a preheated oven at 180°C/350°F/Gas mark 4 for 30–35 minutes until golden. Cut through into the 16 portions again, and serve warm or cold.

••••••••••••••••••••••••••••••••••

Cauliflower and cheese flan

Serves 8

PASTRY

6oz/175g fine wholemeal self-raising flour

2½oz/65g sunflower margarine

1 rounded tablespoon grated Parmesan cheese

½ teaspoon mustard powder

water

FILLING

12oz/350g cauliflower, cut into tiny florets

8oz/225g cottage cheese

1½oz/40g Cheddar cheese, grated

6 spring onions, trimmed and finely sliced

1 egg, beaten

1 rounded tablespoon fromage frais

1 teaspoon chives

black pepper

parsley

Mix the mustard powder with the flour, and rub in the margarine. Stir in the Parmesan and add enough water to bind. Turn out onto a floured board and roll out to fit a greased loose-bottomed 8in/20cm diameter flan tin. Prick the base and bake blind in a preheated oven at 170°C/325°F/Gas mark 3 for 5 minutes.

Steam the cauliflower until just tender. Mix the cottage cheese with the Cheddar, onions, egg, fromage frais and chives. Add the cauliflower and season with black pepper. Mix well and spoon evenly into the pastry flan case. Sprinkle the top with parsley and return to the oven. Bake for about 35 minutes until set.

Cut into 8 equal portions and serve either warm or cold.

Broccoli and spinach flan

Serves 8

PASTRY

As for Cauliflower and cheese flan
(see opposite)

FILLING

10oz/300g broccoli

4oz/100g frozen cooked chopped
spinach, thawed

2oz/50g Cheddar cheese, grated

1 onion, peeled and chopped

1 garlic clove, crushed

1 egg, beaten

1 rounded tablespoon natural
yoghurt

1 dessertspoon vegetable oil

1 teaspoon chervil

pinch of ground bay leaves

black pepper

Make up the pastry flan case
exactly as for Cauliflower and
cheese flan (see opposite).

Chop the broccoli into small pieces
and steam until just tender. Heat
the oil and gently fry the onion and
garlic until softened. Remove from
the heat and add the steamed
broccoli and remaining filling
ingredients. Mix thoroughly, then
spoon the filling evenly into the
pastry flan case. Return to the oven
and bake for about 35 minutes until
set.

Cut into 8 equal portions and serve
warm or cold.

Sweetcorn and watercress flan

Serves 8

PASTRY

6oz/175g fine wholemeal self-
raising flour

2½oz/65g sunflower margarine

½ teaspoon mustard powder

water

FILLING

8oz/225g frozen sweetcorn kernels

1 bunch of watercress, trimmed
and chopped

1 small onion, peeled and finely
chopped

2 eggs, beaten

1 dessertspoon vegetable oil

1 teaspoon chervil

1 teaspoon chives

black pepper

Mix the mustard powder with the
flour and rub in the margarine.
Add enough water to bind and turn
out onto a floured board. Roll out
to fit a greased loose-bottomed
8in/20cm diameter flan tin. Prick
the base and bake blind in a
preheated oven at 170°C/325°F/
Gas mark 3 for 5 minutes.

Cook the sweetcorn, then drain
and put 2oz/50g aside. Heat the oil
and gently fry the onion until soft.
Remove from the heat and add the
6oz/175g sweetcorn together with
the remaining filling ingredients.
Blend until smooth, then stir in the

reserved sweetcorn kernels. Pour evenly into the pastry flan case. Return to the oven and bake for about 35 minutes until set.

Cut into 8 equal portions and serve warm or cold.

....

Asparagus, ricotta and walnut flan

Serves 8

PASTRY

As for Sweetcorn and watercress flan (page 00)

FILLING

12oz/350g asparagus

8oz/225g ricotta cheese

1½oz/40g walnuts

4 spring onions, trimmed and finely sliced

1 egg, beaten

2 rounded tablespoons natural set yoghurt

1 teaspoon parsley

½ teaspoon mustard powder

¼ teaspoon grated nutmeg

black pepper

Make up the pastry flan case exactly as for the Sweetcorn and watercress flan (see page 27).

Cut the tips off the asparagus. Cut the stems in half lengthwise if thick, then cut them into ½in/1cm lengths. Steam the chopped stems and tips until just tender. Reserve the tips and put the stems in a mixing bowl.

Keep a few walnuts aside and grate the rest. Add the grated walnuts to the bowl together with the ricotta, spring onions, egg, yoghurt, parsley, mustard, nutmeg and black pepper. Mix thoroughly and spoon evenly into the pastry case.

Arrange the asparagus tips on the top and press in lightly. Chop the reserved walnuts and sprinkle them over the top. Return to the oven and bake for about 35 minutes until set.

Cut into 8 equal portions and serve warm or cold.

....

Apricot and pistachio strudel

Serves 9

12 12x8in/30x20cm sheets of filo pastry

8oz/225g fresh apricots, stoned and finely chopped

4oz/100g shelled pistachios, chopped

4oz/100g mixed long grain and wild rice

2 sticks of celery, trimmed and finely chopped

1 onion, peeled and finely chopped

12 fl.oz/350ml water

1 egg, beaten

1 tablespoon sunflower oil

1 teaspoon soy sauce

1 teaspoon chervil

½ teaspoon ground coriander

¼ teaspoon paprika

black pepper

extra sunflower oil

sesame seeds

Heat the tablespoon of oil and gently fry the onion and celery for 10 minutes. Add the rice and fry for 2 minutes more. Add the apricots, water and soy sauce and bring to the boil. Cover and simmer very gently until the liquid has been absorbed and the rice is tender. Remove from the heat and allow to cool. Add the pistachios, egg, chervil, coriander and paprika and season with black pepper. Mix thoroughly and set aside.

Lay a sheet of filo pastry onto a sheet of cling film and brush with sunflower oil. Lay a second sheet of filo on top of this one, brush with oil and lay a third sheet of filo on top. Spread one third of the filling evenly over the pastry leaving a 1in/2½cm border along the two long edges. Repeat these pastry and filling layers twice and finish with 3 more sheets of pastry.

Fold the long edges of pastry towards the centre and carefully transfer with the join underneath to a greased baking sheet. Brush with sunflower oil and sprinkle with sesame seeds.

Bake in a preheated oven at 180°C/ 350°F/Gas mark 4 for 35–40 minutes until golden and crispy. Transfer to a serving plate and cut into 9 slices. Serve warm or cold.

....
Celeriac and cheese pastry ring

Serves 8–10

8oz/225g puff pastry

1lb/450g celeriac, peeled and grated

4oz/100g cottage cheese, mashed

2oz/50g Edam cheese, grated

1 onion, peeled and finely chopped

1 tablespoon vegetable oil

black pepper

1 rounded teaspoon chives

1 rounded teaspoon parsley

½ teaspoon mustard powder

milk

sesame seeds and onion seeds

Heat the oil in a large saucepan and gently fry the onion until softened. Add the celeriac and cook for 2–3 minutes whilst stirring. Remove from the heat and add the cottage cheese, Edam, chives, parsley and mustard powder. Season with black pepper and mix thoroughly.

Roll out the pastry on a piece of floured cling film to an oblong shape measuring 24x8in/61x20cm. Spread the celeriac mixture lengthwise evenly along one half of the pastry, leaving a ½in/1cm strip along the edge for joining. Dampen the edge with milk and fold the pastry over to enclose the filling. Press the pastry edges together using a fork. ➔

29

Carefully transfer the roll onto a greased baking sheet, shaping it into a circle. Pinch the pastry on top in a random pattern to decorate. Prick the top with a fork and brush with milk. Sprinkle with the sesame and onion seeds.

Bake in a preheated oven at 170°C/325°F/Gas mark 3 for about 35 minutes until golden. Allow to cool slightly, then carefully transfer to a serving plate. Cut into slices and serve warm or cold.

Ricotta and spinach tarts

Makes 18

PASTRY

12oz/350g fine wholemeal self-raising flour

4oz/100g sunflower margarine

2 rounded tablespoons grated Parmesan cheese

2 teaspoons mustard powder

milk

FILLING

1lb/450g ricotta cheese

8oz/225g frozen cooked chopped spinach, thawed

8 spring onions, trimmed and finely sliced

2 eggs, beaten

4 fl.oz/125ml milk

2 teaspoons chervil

½ teaspoon grated nutmeg

black pepper

Rub the margarine into the flour. Stir in the Parmesan and mustard powder. Add enough milk to bind, then turn out onto a floured board. Divide the pastry into 18 pieces of equal size. Roll out each piece of pastry to fit a 2¾in/7cm diameter greased muffin tin. Prick the bases and bake blind in a preheated oven at 180°C/350°F/Gas mark 4 for 5 minutes.

Put the spinach in a sieve and press out any water. Transfer the spinach to a mixing bowl and add the remaining filling ingredients. Mix thoroughly, then spoon into the pastry cases. Return to the oven and bake for 30–35 minutes until set. Slide a sharp knife around the edge to loosen. Carefully remove the tarts from the tins and serve warm or cold.

Mushroom, millet and almond boats

Makes 16

PASTRY

5oz/150g fine wholemeal self-raising flour

1oz/25g ground almonds

2½oz/65g sunflower margarine

water

FILLING

4oz/100g mushrooms, wiped and finely chopped

2oz/50g ground almonds

2oz/50g millet

6 fl.oz/175ml water

1 small onion, peeled and finely chopped

1 tablespoon sherry

1 teaspoon yeast extract

1 dessertspoon sunflower oil

1 teaspoon parsley

1 teaspoon thyme

black pepper

1 egg, beaten

flaked almonds

First make the pastry. Mix the flour with the ground almonds and rub in the margarine. Add enough water to bind, then turn out onto a floured board. Roll out thinly and line 16 boat-shaped tins. To get the exact shape, use an upturned boat tin as a template to cut round. Prick the bases and bake blind for 5 minutes in a preheated oven at 180°C/350°F/Gas mark 4.

Put the millet, water, sherry and yeast extract in a saucepan and bring to the boil. Stir well to dissolve the yeast extract, then cover and simmer gently until the liquid has been absorbed.

Heat the oil in another pan and gently fry the onion until softened. Add the mushrooms and fry for a further 2 minutes. Remove from the heat and add the cooked millet, ground almonds, egg, parsley and thyme. Season with black pepper and mix well. Spoon the filling into the pastry cases and arrange some flaked almonds neatly on the tops.

Return to the oven and bake for about 25 minutes until golden. Serve warm or cold.

....

Blue cheese, mushroom and parsley squares

Makes 32

PASTRY

8oz/225g fine wholemeal self-raising flour

3oz/75g sunflower margarine

1 teaspoon mustard powder

milk

TOPPING

8oz/225g mushrooms, wiped and finely chopped

4oz/100g dolcelatte cheese, mashed

2oz/50g fresh parsley, finely chopped

2oz/50g fresh wholemeal bread-crumbs

1 onion, peeled and finely chopped

2 eggs, beaten

1 tablespoon sunflower oil

black pepper

½ teaspoon cayenne pepper

1 teaspoon thyme

1 teaspoon oregano

fresh parsley sprigs

Sift the flour with the mustard powder. Rub in the margarine and add enough milk to bind. Turn out onto a floured board and divide into two. Roll out each piece to an 8in/20cm square. ➔

Line the bases of 2 lined and greased 8in/20cm square flan tins with the pastry. Prick the bases and bake blind in a preheated oven at 180°C/350°F/Gas mark 4 for 5 minutes.

Heat the oil and gently fry the onion until softened. Add the mushrooms and fry for 2 minutes. Remove from the heat and add the dolcelatte, chopped parsley, breadcrumbs, eggs, cayenne pepper, thyme and oregano and season with black pepper. Mix thoroughly and divide the mixture between the pastry bases. Spread out evenly and return to the oven for 40–45 minutes until golden.

Allow to cool slightly, then cut each flan into 16 equal squares. Transfer to a serving plate and garnish with the fresh parsley sprigs. Serve warm or cold.

Courgette and spinach fingers

Makes 16

- 8oz/225g puff pastry
- 8oz/225g courgettes, grated
- 8oz/225g frozen cooked chopped spinach, thawed
- 2oz/50g mixed nuts, grated
- 2oz/50g fresh wholemeal breadcrumbs
- 1 onion, peeled and finely chopped
- 1 egg, beaten
- 1 teaspoon marjoram
- 1 teaspoon thyme
- pinch of ground bay leaves
- black pepper
- milk
- onion seeds

Put the spinach in a fine sieve and press out excess water. Transfer the spinach to a mixing bowl and add the courgettes, nuts, breadcrumbs, onion, egg, marjoram, thyme, and ground bay leaves. Add black pepper to taste, and mix thoroughly.

Cut the pastry in half and roll out each piece to an 11x7in/28x18cm oblong. Line a baking tin of the same size and grease. Put one of the pieces of pastry in the tin, spread the filling evenly over the pastry, and lay the other pastry sheet on top. Press down lightly. Using a sharp knife, cut into quarters and then cut each quarter into 4 fingers, making 16 fingers in all. Lightly score the top with a sharp knife in a zigzag pattern. Brush with milk and sprinkle with onion seeds.

Bake in a preheated oven at 170°C/325°F/Gas mark 3 for 35–40 minutes until golden. Cut through into fingers again and transfer to a serving plate. Serve warm or cold.

Mushroom and hazelnut choux buns

Makes 12

PASTRY

2½oz/65g plain wholewheat flour

2oz/50g vegetable margarine

5fl.oz/150ml water

2 eggs, beaten

¼ teaspoon cayenne pepper

FILLING

4oz/100g mushrooms, wiped and finely chopped

2oz/50g hazelnuts, grated

2oz/50g Cheddar cheese, grated

1 small onion, peeled and grated

1 dessertspoon vegetable oil

2 teaspoons chervil

black pepper

Put the margarine and water in a saucepan and bring to the boil to melt the margarine. Remove from the heat and beat in the sifted flour and cayenne pepper, using a wooden spoon. Heat while stirring until a soft ball forms. Remove from the heat and allow to cool slightly. Beat in one egg at a time and mix until the mixture is smooth and shiny. Divide the mixture between 12 holes of a greased and floured tart tin. Bake in a preheated oven at 180°C/350°F/Gas mark 4 for 15 minutes, until well risen.

Meanwhile, make the filling. Heat the oil and gently fry the onion until softened. Add the mushrooms and fry for a couple of minutes, whilst stirring. Remove from the heat and add the remaining filling ingredients. Mix together well. Slit the choux buns and fill each of them with some of the filling. Return to the oven for 10–15 minutes until golden. Serve warm or cold.

Cheese and pineapple tarts

Makes 24

PASTRY

6oz/175g fine wholemeal self-raising flour

2oz/50g sunflower margarine

½ teaspoon mustard powder

1 rounded tablespoon grated Parmesan cheese

water

FILLING

6oz/175g cottage cheese

2oz/50g Edam cheese, grated

2oz/50g fresh wholemeal breadcrumbs

4 tinned pineapple rings

1 onion, peeled and finely chopped

1 egg, beaten

black pepper

¼ teaspoon cayenne pepper

1 teaspoon chives

1 teaspoon chervil

1 tablespoon grated Parmesan cheese

sesame seeds ➔

33

First make the pastry. Mix the mustard powder and Parmesan with the flour. Rub in the margarine and add enough water to bind. Turn out onto a floured board and roll out thinly. Cut into 24 circles using a 2½in/6cm pastry cutter. Place the pastry circles in greased tart tins, prick the bases and bake blind in a preheated oven at 170°C/ 325°F/Gas mark 3 for 5 minutes.

Pat the pineapple rings on kitchen paper to dry slightly, then chop finely and put in a mixing bowl with the remaining filling ingredients, except the sesame seeds. Mix thoroughly, then divide the mixture between the 24 pastry bases. Sprinkle the tops with sesame seeds and return to the oven. Bake for about 30 minutes till golden. Serve warm or cold.

....

Watercress and mushroom baskets

Makes 20

The pastry baskets can be made the day before required and stored in an airtight container. The filling can be made several hours in advance and refrigerated. Fill the baskets just before serving.

10 12x8in/30x20cm sheets of filo pastry

8oz/225g mushrooms, wiped and finely chopped

8oz/225g cottage cheese, mashed

1 bunch of watercress, finely chopped

8 spring onions, trimmed and finely sliced

1 tablespoon olive oil

black pepper

2 teaspoons chives

2 teaspoons thyme

sunflower oil

chopped fresh parsley

Cut the pastry sheets into 4x4in/10x10cm squares. Take one pastry square and brush lightly with sunflower oil. Place another sheet on top, offsetting the points, and again brush lightly with sunflower oil. Place another sheet of pastry on top, offsetting the points again so that a pointed star shape is achieved. Press this shape into a 3in/8cm diameter muffin tin and brush lightly with oil. Repeat with the other pastry squares so that 20 little pastry baskets are made.

Bake in a preheated oven at 190°C/375°F/Gas mark 5 for 8–10 minutes until golden. Transfer to a wire rack and allow to cool.

Heat the olive oil and gently fry the mushrooms for 2 minutes whilst stirring. Allow to cool, then refrigerate until cold. When cold, add the cottage cheese, watercress, spring onions, chives and thyme and season with black pepper. Mix until well combined. Divide the mixture between the pastry baskets and serve garnished with chopped fresh parsley.

Split pea and pepper pouches

Makes 12

10oz/300g puff pastry

4oz/100g split yellow peas

6oz/175g mixed peppers (i.e. green, red, orange), finely chopped

6 spring onions, trimmed and finely sliced

2 garlic cloves, crushed

1 rounded tablespoon natural yoghurt

1 dessertspoon olive oil

1 rounded teaspoon chervil

1 rounded teaspoon marjoram

½ teaspoon mustard powder

black pepper

few drops of tabasco sauce

milk

Soak the split peas overnight, rinse and place in a fresh pan of water. Bring to the boil, cover and simmer for about an hour until tender. Drain and mash. Heat the oil and gently fry the chopped peppers, onion and garlic for 10 minutes. Remove from the heat and add the mashed peas, yoghurt, chervil, marjoram, mustard and tabasco sauce. Season with black pepper and mix thoroughly. Set aside and allow to cool.

Divide the pastry into 12 equal pieces. Roll each piece into a ball in the palm of your hand, then roll out into a 5in/13cm circle. Divide the filling equally between the circles. Gather the pastry edges up towards the top to make pouch shapes, and pinch together to join. Prick each side of the pouches with a fork, and brush all over with milk.

Bake in a preheated oven at 170°C/325°F/Gas mark 3 for about 40 minutes until golden. Serve warm or cold.

Pineapple, date and walnut pasties

Makes 12

12oz/350g puff pastry

6 tinned pineapple slices

4oz/100g dried dates, chopped

4oz/100g cottage cheese

2oz/50g Cheddar cheese, grated

2oz/50g walnuts, grated

1 small onion, peeled and finely chopped

black pepper

2 teaspoons chives

½ teaspoon grated nutmeg

milk

poppy seeds

Divide the pastry equally into 12 and roll each piece into a ball in the palm of your hand, then roll out on a floured board into a 5½in/14cm diameter circle.

Pat the pineapple dry on kitchen paper, then chop finely. Put the pineapple in a mixing bowl with the dates, cottage cheese, Cheddar, walnuts and onion. Add the chives and nutmeg and season with black pepper. Mix thoroughly, then divide the mixture between the 12 pastry circles. Brush the edges with milk and bring the pastry sides up to join on the top to make pasty shapes. Crimp the edges together to secure and make a slit in each side. Brush with milk and sprinkle with poppy seeds.

Bake in a preheated oven at 170°C/325°F/Gas mark 3 for about 35 minutes until golden. Serve warm or cold.

....

Spiced chestnut and carrot rolls

Makes 16

6 20x10in/50x25cm sheets of filo pastry

8oz/225g shelled chestnuts, grated

8oz/225g carrots, scraped and grated

4oz/100g celery, trimmed and finely chopped

1oz/25g raisins, chopped

1 onion, peeled and finely chopped

1 egg, beaten

1 tablespoon sunflower oil

1 dessertspoon soy sauce

1 rounded teaspoon ground coriander

1 teaspoon ground cumin

½ teaspoon grated nutmeg

black pepper

extra sunflower oil

onion seeds

Heat the tablespoonful of sunflower oil and gently fry the onion and celery for 10 minutes. Remove from the heat and add the chestnuts, carrot, raisins, egg, soy sauce, coriander, cumin and nutmeg. Season with black pepper. Mix thoroughly and set aside.

Lay one of the filo sheets out flat and brush lightly with sunflower oil. Lay a second sheet on top and again brush lightly with sunflower oil. Lay a third sheet on top and cut all three into eight 5in/12½cm squares. Repeat these instructions with the other 3 filo sheets.

Divide the filling mixture between the 16 squares, placing it evenly in the centres. Fold the pastry edges towards the centre to enclose the filling completely. Dampen the edges with milk where they meet and place the rolls with the joins underneath on a greased baking sheet. Brush the rolls lightly with sunflower oil and sprinkle with the onion seeds.

Bake in a preheated oven at 180°C/350°F/Gas mark 4 for 25–30 minutes until golden and crispy. Serve warm or cold.

Smoky mushroom and potato pinwheels

Makes 16

PASTRY

8oz/225g fine wholemeal self-raising flour

2oz/50g sunflower margarine

1 teaspoon mustard powder

1 rounded tablespoon grated Parmesan cheese

milk

FILLING

8oz/225g potato, peeled

4oz/100g mushrooms, wiped and finely chopped

2oz/50g smoked Cheddar cheese, grated

1 small onion, peeled and finely chopped

1 tablespoon sunflower oil

black pepper

1 teaspoon parsley

1 teaspoon chervil

poppy seeds

Cut the potato into even-sized chunks and put in a pan of water. Bring to the boil and boil for 5 minutes. Drain and allow to cool. Heat the oil and gently fry the onion until softened. Add the mushrooms and fry for 2 minutes. Remove from the heat and allow to cool. Grate the potato and add to the mushroom mixture together with the smoked cheese, parsley and chervil. Season with black pepper and mix thoroughly.

Mix the mustard powder with the flour and rub in the margarine. Stir in the Parmesan and add enough milk to bind. Turn out onto a floured board and knead. Roll out on a piece of floured cling film to an oblong shape measuring 14x9in/35x23cm.

Spread the filling evenly over the pastry using a palette knife. Leave a 1in/2½cm gap along one of the long edges. Starting at the other long edge, roll up tightly like a Swiss roll by pulling up the cling film. Dampen the exposed edge with milk to join. Using a sharp knife, cut the roll into 16 equal slices. Lay the slices flat on a greased baking sheet and sprinkle them with poppy seeds.

Bake in a preheated oven at 180°C/350°F/Gas mark 4 for 35–40 minutes till golden. Serve hot.

Cheesy spinach and pecan parcels

Makes 12

8oz/225g puff pastry

4oz/100g frozen cooked chopped spinach, thawed

4oz/100g cottage cheese, mashed

2oz/50g Cheddar cheese, grated

2oz/50g pecans, grated

1 small onion, peeled and grated

black pepper

½ teaspoon ground mace

2 teaspoons chives ➔

milk

poppy seeds

Put the spinach in a fine sieve and press out any excess water. Transfer to a mixing bowl and add the cottage cheese, Cheddar, pecans, onion, ground mace and chives. Season with black pepper, mix well, and set aside.

Cut the pastry in half and roll out each piece to an oblong shape measuring 12x8in/30x20cm. Cut each piece into six 4x4in/10x10cm squares.

Divide the filling between the 12 pastry squares, placing it carefully in the centre of each. Dampen the edges of each square with milk. Join all four corners of each square on the top to make parcel shapes. Crimp the edges together to join. Brush with milk and sprinkle with poppy seeds.

Place the parcels on a greased baking sheet and bake in a preheated oven at 170°C/325°F/ Gas mark 3 for 35–40 minutes until golden. Transfer to a serving plate and serve warm or cold.

Savoury filled vol-au-vents

Use medium-size ready made frozen vol-au-vent cases. Cook according to the instructions on the packet. They can be baked the day before required, allowed to cool on a wire rack, then stored in an airtight container. Fill just before serving.

Each filling given below fills 12 medium-size vol-au-vents. All can be made several hours before required and refrigerated (except the Avocado, tomato and parsley filling, which needs to be made no more than 2 hours before serving to prevent the avocado from discolouring).

Mozzarella salad filling

4oz/100g tomatoes, skinned and finely chopped

2oz/50g red pepper

2oz/50g green pepper

2oz/50g mushrooms

2oz/50g mozzarella cheese, grated

2 spring onions, trimmed and finely sliced

1 garlic clove, crushed

1 dessertspoon tomato purée

1 teaspoon oregano

½ teaspoon basil

black pepper

Put the tomatoes in a small saucepan and heat gently until

pulpy. Remove from the heat and allow to cool, then refrigerate until cold.

Finely chop the red and green peppers and the mushrooms and add to the tomatoes, together with the remaining ingredients. Mix thoroughly.

Water chestnut and cranberry filling

8oz/225g tin water chestnuts
4oz/100g cranberry sauce
2 spring onions, trimmed and finely chopped
black pepper

Drain the water chestnuts and grate them. Add the remaining ingredients and mix thoroughly.

Avocado, tomato and parsley filling

1 avocado pear
4oz/100g tomatoes, skinned and finely chopped
½ oz/15g fresh parsley, finely chopped
2 teaspoons lemon juice
black pepper

Mash the avocado flesh with the lemon juice. Add the remaining ingredients and mix well.

Avoid making more than 2 hours before required, or the avocado will discolour.

Curried sweetcorn and curd cheese filling

6oz/175g frozen sweetcorn kernels
4oz/100g low-fat curd cheese
4 spring onions, trimmed and finely chopped
1 teaspoon sunflower oil
½ teaspoon curry powder
¼ teaspoon turmeric
¼ teaspoon ground coriander
black pepper

Cook the sweetcorn kernels, then drain. Heat the oil and gently fry the spring onions until softened. Add the curry powder, turmeric and ground coriander and fry for 1 minute while stirring. Remove from the heat and add the drained sweetcorn. Allow to cool, then refrigerate until cold.

When cold, add the curd cheese and season with black pepper. Mix thoroughly.

Egg and watercress filling

4 hardboiled eggs
½ bunch of watercress, finely chopped
4oz/100g quark
1 rounded teaspoon chives
black pepper

Chop the eggs whilst still warm, then mash them with a potato masher. Add the remaining ingredients and mix thoroughly.

Aubergine and hazelnut filling

12oz/350g aubergine, very finely
  chopped
2oz/50g hazelnuts, grated
1 garlic clove, crushed
2 tablespoons olive oil
2 tablespoons sherry
1 rounded tablespoon quark
1 teaspoon soy sauce
1 teaspoon parsley
1 teaspoon chives
black pepper

Heat the oil and gently fry the
aubergine and garlic for about
12–15 minutes until soft. Stir
frequently to prevent sticking. Add
the sherry and soy sauce and cook
for a further 2 minutes. Remove
from the heat and allow to cool,
then refrigerate until cold. When
cold add the remaining ingredients
and mix thoroughly.

PATÉS AND
SAVOURY LOAVES

VEGETABLES, fruits, nuts, grains and pulses lend themselves perfectly to making tasty and interesting patés and savoury loaves. Grouped together under this heading you will find recipes for making bowls of paté suitable for spreading onto savoury biscuits or breads, individual portions of paté made in small ramekin dishes, and lastly savoury loaves for cutting into slices to serve.

All the recipes in this section can either be made the day before, allowed to cool, then covered and refrigerated until required, or they can be made longer in advance and frozen.

Some of the patés are delicious served either warm or cold, and this is indicated in the recipes. To serve a paté warm, simply cover it with foil and place in a preheated oven 170°C/ 325°F/Gas mark 3 for about 15–20 minutes (a little longer from frozen) until warmed through.

Chutneys and salads make ideal accompaniments for all the patés. The savoury loaves look very attractive when served on oblong plates and surrounded by mixed salad leaves.

If you intend serving bowls of spreading paté, remember to provide plenty of savoury biscuits and breads. Such paté also makes an excellent filling for sandwiches.

Aubergine, fennel and mushroom paté

Serves 9

1lb/450g aubergine, finely chopped
8oz/225g fennel bulb, finely chopped
8oz/225g mushrooms, wiped and finely chopped
1 onion, peeled and finely chopped
2 garlic cloves, crushed
4oz/100g fresh wholemeal bread-crumbs
1 egg, beaten
2 rounded tablespoons grated Parmesan cheese
2 tablespoons olive oil
1 tablespoon white wine
black pepper
2 teaspoons basil
2 teaspoons parsley
fresh basil leaves

Heat the oil and gently fry the aubergine, fennel, onion and garlic for about 10 minutes until softened. Stir frequently to prevent sticking. Add the mushrooms and cook for a further minute. Remove from the heat and add the remaining ingredients, except the fresh basil. Mix thoroughly, then spoon the mixture into a greased 10x7in/25x18cm ovenproof dish. Level the top.

Bake in a preheated oven at 180°C/350°F/Gas mark 4 for 45–50 minutes till golden. Allow to cool, cover and refrigerate. Serve cold, garnished with the fresh basil leaves.

Carrot and caraway paté

Serves 8

1lb/450g carrots, scraped and grated
4oz/100g cottage cheese, mashed
2oz/50g dried dates, finely chopped
2oz/50g mixed nuts, grated
2oz/50g fresh wholemeal bread-crumbs
1 onion, peeled and finely chopped
1 egg, beaten
1 tablespoon sunflower oil
2 teaspoons caraway seeds
1 teaspoon chives
¼ teaspoon dill weed
black pepper
sesame seeds

Heat the oil and gently fry the onion and carrot for 5 minutes. Remove from the heat and add the remaining ingredients, except the sesame seeds.

Mix thoroughly and spoon the mixture into a greased 8in/20cm diameter ovenproof dish. Press down firmly and level the top. Sprinkle with sesame seeds and bake in a preheated oven at 180°C/350°F/Gas mark 4 for 40 minutes until golden.

Serve warm or cold.

Curried courgette, apple and nut paté

Serves 8

8oz/225g courgettes, grated

8oz/225g cooking apples, peeled, cored and grated

2oz/50g ground almonds

2oz/50g fresh wholemeal bread-crumbs

1oz/25g Brazil nuts, grated

1oz/25g walnuts, grated

1 onion, peeled and finely chopped

1 garlic clove, crushed

1 teaspoon medium curry powder

1 teaspoon ground coriander

¼ teaspoon turmeric

black pepper

1 dessertspoon vegetable oil

1 tablespoon chopped fresh coriander leaves

1 egg, beaten

1 tablespoon flaked almonds

Heat the oil in a large saucepan and gently fry the onion and garlic until softened. Add the curry powder, coriander and turmeric and fry for a few seconds longer. Remove from the heat and add the remaining ingredients, except for the flaked almonds. Mix thoroughly, spoon into a greased 8in/20cm diameter ovenproof dish and press down firmly and evenly. Sprinkle the flaked almonds over the top, press them in lightly, and cover with foil.

Bake in a preheated oven at 180°C/350°F/Gas mark 4 for 40 minutes. Remove the foil and return to the oven for a further 15–20 minutes until golden. Allow to cool. Serve warm or cold in the dish.

Mixed lentil and leek paté

Serves 9

1lb/450g leeks, trimmed and finely chopped

2oz/50g red lentils

2oz/50g brown lentils

2oz/50g green lentils

2oz/50g fresh wholemeal bread-crumbs

2oz/50g mixed nuts, grated

2 garlic cloves, crushed

1 rounded tablespoon fromage frais

1 tablespoon sunflower oil

1 rounded teaspoon thyme

1 rounded teaspoon mixed herbs

1 teaspoon yeast extract

black pepper

1 egg

sesame seeds

Soak the lentils in water overnight. Drain, rinse well and put in a large pan of fresh water. Bring to the boil, cover and simmer for about 25 minutes until tender. Drain in a sieve and set aside.

Heat the oil in a large saucepan and gently fry the leek and garlic for 5 minutes.

Remove from the heat and add the drained lentils. Beat the egg with the fromage frais and yeast extract. Add to the mixture together with the remaining ingredients, except the sesame seeds. Mix thoroughly, then spoon the mixture into a greased 10x7in/25x18cm oven-proof dish. Level the top and sprinkle with sesame seeds. Bake in a preheated oven at 180°C/350°F/Gas mark 4 for 30 minutes. Serve warm or cold.

Spiced potted mushrooms with hazelnuts

Makes 12

1lb/450g mushrooms, wiped and finely chopped

8oz/225g red lentils

4oz/100g hazelnuts, grated

2oz/50g fresh wholemeal bread-crumbs

1 onion, peeled and finely chopped

2 garlic cloves, crushed

1 tablespoon vegetable oil

2 eggs, beaten

1 dessertspoon soy sauce

2 rounded teaspoons ground coriander

2 rounded teaspoons ground cumin

½ teaspoon cayenne pepper

black pepper

6 hazelnuts, halved

Cook the lentils until tender, then drain in a fine sieve and press out excess liquid using the back of a spoon. Heat the oil and gently fry the onion and garlic until softened. Add the coriander, cumin and cayenne pepper and fry for 1 minute. Add the mushrooms and fry for a further 2 minutes whilst stirring. Remove from the heat and add the drained lentils, grated hazelnuts, breadcrumbs, eggs and soy sauce and season with black pepper. Mix thoroughly.

Divide the mixture between 12 3in/8cm ramekin dishes. Press down evenly and place a hazelnut half on each. Bake in a preheated oven at 180°C/350°F/Gas mark 4 for 45 minutes until golden. Serve warm or cold in the dishes.

Mung bean and courgette paté pots

Makes 12

8oz/225g mung beans

1lb/450g courgettes, grated

1 onion, peeled and finely chopped

4 garlic cloves, crushed

1 tablespoon olive oil

4oz/100g fresh wholemeal bread-crumbs

2 eggs, beaten

2 teaspoons marjoram

1 teaspoon thyme

1 teaspoon rosemary ➧

black pepper
fresh parsley sprigs

Soak the mung beans overnight. Rinse and place in a fresh pan of water. Bring to the boil, cover and simmer for about 40 minutes until tender. Drain thoroughly and mash with a potato masher.

Heat the oil in a large saucepan and gently fry the onion and garlic until softened. Remove from the heat and add the mashed beans and remaining ingredients, except the parsley sprigs. Mix thoroughly. Divide the mixture between 12 3in/8cm ramekin dishes, and press down evenly.

Bake in a preheated oven at 180°C/ 350°F/Gas mark 4 for 40–45 minutes until golden. Garnish the top of each ramekin with a small sprig of fresh parsley. Serve in the dishes, either warm or cold.

Carrot, buckwheat and walnut paté wrapped in spinach

Makes 12

1lb/450g carrots, scraped and grated
6oz/175g fresh spinach
4oz/100g roasted buckwheat
4oz/100g walnuts, grated
1 onion, peeled and finely chopped
2 eggs, beaten

12 fl.oz/350ml water
1 tablespoon sunflower oil
2 teaspoons soy sauce
1 teaspoon paprika
½ teaspoon cayenne pepper
½ teaspoon yeast extract
black pepper
1 small carrot, scraped and grated

Heat the oil in a large saucepan and gently fry the onion until softened. Add the 1lb/450g carrots and the buckwheat and fry for 1 minute. Add the water, soy sauce and yeast extract and stir well. Bring to the boil, then cover and simmer gently for about 10 minutes until the liquid has been absorbed. Remove from the heat and add the remaining ingredients, except the spinach and small grated carrot. Mix thoroughly and set aside.

Remove any thick stalks from the spinach and discard. Plunge the spinach into boiling water for a few seconds, then drain well. Use the spinach to line 12 greased 3in/8cm ramekin dishes. Reserve some of the leaves for covering the tops.

Divide the paté mixture between the 12 lined dishes and press down evenly. Cover the tops with more spinach leaves, then transfer the dishes to a baking sheet and cover with foil.

Bake in a preheated oven at 190°C/ 375°F/Gas mark 5 for 35–40 minutes. Allow to cool in the dishes for 15 minutes, then invert onto a serving plate. Refrigerate for a few hours until cold.

To serve, garnish the tops with a little grated carrot.

Aubergine, pecan and brown rice ramekins

Makes 12

1lb/450g aubergine, finely chopped

8oz/225g long grain brown rice

4oz/100g pecans, grated

1 onion, peeled and finely chopped

2 garlic cloves, crushed

2 eggs, beaten

4 rounded tablespoons grated Parmesan cheese

2 tablespoons olive oil

2 tablespoons tomato purée

1 tablespoon Worcester sauce

2 teaspoons parsley

1 teaspoon basil

1 teaspoon oregano

black pepper

12 pecan halves

Cook the rice until tender, then drain. Heat the oil in a large saucepan and gently fry the onion, garlic and aubergine for about 10 minutes until soft. Stir frequently to prevent sticking. Remove from the heat and stir in the cooked rice together with the remaining ingredients, except the pecan halves. Mix thoroughly. Divide the

mixture between 12 3in/8cm greased ramekin dishes, and press down firmly and evenly.

Bake in a preheated oven at 180°C/350°F/Gas mark 4 for 30–35 minutes until golden and set. Garnish the top of each ramekin with a pecan half and serve warm or cold.

Celery and buckwheat loaf

Serves 8

12oz/350g celery, trimmed and finely chopped

4oz/100g roasted buckwheat

2oz/50g fresh wholemeal bread-crumbs

1 onion, peeled and finely chopped

10 fl.oz/300ml hot water

2 tablespoons water

1 tablespoon vegetable oil

1 egg, beaten

1 rounded teaspoon yeast extract

1 teaspoon parsley

1 teaspoon chives

black pepper

Dissolve the yeast extract in the 10 fl.oz/300ml hot water and pour into a saucepan with the buckwheat. Bring to the boil, cover, and turn the heat to its lowest setting. Cook for 10 minutes until the liquid has been absorbed. Stir a few times to prevent sticking. ➡

Heat the oil in another saucepan and gently fry the onion and celery for 10 minutes, then blend with the 2 tablespoons of water until smooth. Add the celery purée to the buckwheat, together with the breadcrumbs, egg, parsley and chives, and season with black pepper. Mix thoroughly, then spoon into a base-lined and greased 8in/20cm loaf tin.

Cover with foil and bake in a preheated oven at 180°C/350°F/ Gas mark 4 for 40 minutes. Remove the foil and bake for a further 20 minutes until golden and firm in the centre. Allow to cool in the tin for 30 minutes, then run a sharp knife round the edges to loosen. Turn out onto a serving plate and carefully peel off the lining.

Cut into slices using a sharp knife and serve warm or cold.

·····························

Brown lentil and mushroom loaf

Serves 9

- 8oz/225g brown lentils
- 8oz/225g mushrooms, wiped and finely chopped
- 4oz/100g fresh wholemeal bread-crumbs
- 1 onion, peeled and finely chopped
- 2 garlic cloves, crushed
- 1 tablespoon vegetable oil
- 1 dessertspoon soy sauce
- 1 teaspoon yeast extract
- 1 rounded teaspoon parsley
- 1 rounded teaspoon chives
- 1 teaspoon paprika
- 1 teaspoon celery seeds
- 1 teaspoon mixed herbs
- black pepper
- 1 egg, beaten

Soak the lentils overnight, then drain and put in a fresh pan of water. Bring to the boil, cover and simmer until very soft. Drain well and set aside.

Heat the oil and gently fry the onion and garlic until softened. Add the mushrooms and fry for a further 2 minutes whilst stirring. Remove from the heat, add the drained lentils and remaining ingredients. Mix together thoroughly. Spoon the mixture into a base-lined and greased 9½in/24cm loaf tin, and press down firmly and evenly.

Bake in a preheated oven at 180°C/350°F/Gas mark 4 for 50 minutes. Slide a sharp knife around the edges to loosen and invert onto a greased baking sheet. Carefully remove the base lining and return to the oven for 10 minutes until golden. Transfer to a serving plate and allow to cool. Cut into slices with a sharp knife and serve warm or cold.

Apricot and pistachio rice loaf

Serves 9

- 8oz/225g fresh apricots, stoned and finely chopped
- 4oz/100g shelled pistachios, grated
- 4oz/100g brown basmati rice
- 4oz/100g fresh wholemeal bread-crumbs
- 1 onion, peeled and finely chopped
- 2 garlic cloves, crushed
- 2 eggs, beaten
- 1 tablespoon sunflower oil
- 1 rounded teaspoon ground coriander
- 1 rounded teaspoon ground cumin
- 1/2 teaspoon turmeric
- 2 cardamoms, husked and the seeds separated
- black pepper
- 10 fl.oz/300ml water
- 2 apricots, stoned and sliced

Heat the oil and gently fry the onion and garlic until softened. Add the rice, coriander, cumin, turmeric and cardamom seeds and fry whilst stirring for 2 minutes. Add the water and bring to the boil. Cover and simmer very gently for 20–25 minutes until the water has been absorbed.

Remove from the heat and add the remaining ingredients, except the sliced apricots. Mix thoroughly. Spoon the mixture into a base-lined and greased 9in/23cm loaf tin. Press down firmly and evenly.

Bake in a preheated oven at 180°C/350°F/Gas mark 4 for 45 minutes. Slide a sharp knife round the edges to loosen, then turn out onto a greased baking tray. Remove the base lining and return to the oven for about 10 minutes until golden. Transfer to a wire rack and allow to cool, then refrigerate until cold.

Garnish the loaf with the sliced apricots. Cut into slices to serve.

Vegetable terrine

Serves 10

- 8oz/225g fresh spinach

ORANGE LAYER

- 12oz/350g carrots, scraped and grated
- 8oz/225g celery, trimmed and finely chopped
- 1 onion, peeled and finely chopped
- 1 tablespoon sunflower oil
- 2 fl.oz/50ml water
- 1 egg, beaten
- 2oz/50g bulgar wheat
- 4 fl.oz/125ml boiling water
- 1 teaspoon chervil
- 1 teaspoon paprika
- 1/2 teaspoon caraway seeds
- 1/2 teaspoon yeast extract
- black pepper

GREEN LAYER

- 12oz/350g courgette, grated
- 1 ripe avocado pear, peeled and mashed ➡

1 onion, peeled and finely
chopped

1 egg, beaten

4oz/100g fresh wholemeal bread-
crumbs

4oz/100g frozen cooked chopped
spinach, thawed

2oz/50g Cheddar cheese, grated

1 dessertspoon sunflower oil

1 teaspoon parsley

1 teaspoon thyme

1/4 teaspoon ground bay leaves

black pepper

First make the orange layer.
Dissolve the yeast extract in the
boiling water. Add the bulgar
wheat and leave to stand for 15
minutes. Heat the oil and gently fry
the onion and celery for 10
minutes. Add the 2 fl.oz/50ml
water and bring to the boil. Cover
and simmer for a few minutes until
the liquid evaporates. Allow to cool
slightly, then blend until smooth.
Transfer the mixture to a mixing
bowl and add the remaining ingredients for the orange layer. Mix
thoroughly and set aside.

Heat the oil for the green layer.
Gently fry the onion until softened,
then remove from the heat. Put the
spinach in a fine sieve and press out
excess water. Add the spinach to
the pan, together with the
remaining ingredients for the green
layer. Mix thoroughly and set aside.

Line a 10in/25cm loaf tin with foil,
and grease it. Remove any thick
stalks from the fresh spinach.

Plunge the spinach leaves in boiling
water for a few seconds, then drain
well. Line the prepared loaf tin
with the spinach leaves, reserving
enough to cover the top.

Spoon half the orange mixture into
the spinach-lined tin, spread out
evenly and press down firmly.
Next, spoon half the green mixture
into the tin, then repeat these layers
once more. Fold the spinach leaves
over the filling and finish covering
completely with the remaining
leaves.

Cover with foil and bake in a
preheated oven at 190°C/375°F/
Gas mark 5 for 75 minutes. Allow
to cool in the tin for 30 minutes,
then invert onto a serving plate.
Carefully remove the foil and allow
to cool further before refrigerating.

To serve, arrange some mixed salad
leaves around the terrine, and cut
into slices with a sharp knife.

DIPS

A SELECTION of dips, surrounded by crisp fresh crudités, makes a colourful and appetising addition to the buffet table.

Crudités are easy to prepare – just wash or scrape the vegetables where necessary and cut them into even-sized strips or chunks. Choose from cauliflower and broccoli, cut into small florets; carrot, swede, turnip, celery, courgette, cucumber, fennel, and red, green and orange peppers, cut into strips; baby sweetcorn, button mushrooms, radishes, chicory and other small, firm salad leaves, left whole; and spring onions, trimmed. Garnish the platter with quartered cherry tomatoes, olives and fresh parsley sprigs.

Prepare the crudités up to 2 hours before serving, and refrigerate. Allow 1½lbs/675g mixed vegetables for 8 people.

Peanut and yoghurt dip

Serves 8

- 4 rounded tablespoons peanut butter
- 6 rounded tablespoons natural low-fat yoghurt
- 4oz/100g cottage cheese
- 1 teaspoon Worcester sauce
- dash of soy sauce
- black pepper
- ½oz/15g shelled peanuts, finely chopped

Take all the ingredients except the chopped peanuts and blend till smooth. Transfer to a serving bowl. Cover and refrigerate for a couple of hours.

Sprinkle the chopped nuts on top and serve.

Mushroom and red wine dip

Serves 8

- 12oz/350g mushrooms, wiped and chopped
- 1 onion, peeled and chopped
- 1 tablespoon olive oil
- 2 garlic cloves, crushed
- 5 fl.oz/150ml red wine
- black pepper
- 1 teaspoon soy sauce
- 1 teaspoon thyme
- 2 teaspoons parsley
- chopped fresh chives

Heat the oil and gently fry the onion and garlic for 10 minutes. Add the mushrooms and fry for 2 minutes whilst stirring. Remove from the heat and allow to cool.

When cool, add the wine, soy sauce, thyme and parsley and season with black pepper. Blend until smooth, then transfer to a serving bowl. Cover and chill for a few hours.

Serve garnished with chopped fresh chives.

Avocado and tomato dip

Serves 8

- 2 ripe avocado pears, peeled and chopped
- 6oz/175g ripe tomatoes, skinned and chopped
- 4 spring onions, trimmed and chopped
- 1 garlic clove, crushed
- 1 tablespoon lemon juice
- 1 tablespoon olive oil
- 1 teaspoon parsley
- black pepper

Blend all the ingredients together until smooth. Put in a serving bowl, cover and refrigerate. To prevent the dip from discolouring, avoid making more than 2 hours before serving.

Watercress and yoghurt dip

Serves 8

  1 bunch of watercress, very finely
    chopped
  8oz/225g cottage cheese, mashed
  5oz/150g natural low-fat set
    yoghurt
  black pepper
  1 teaspoon chives

Mix all the ingredients until well combined. Transfer to a serving bowl. Cover and refrigerate for a couple of hours.

Curried bean and onion dip

Serves 8

  8oz/225g cooked butter beans
  8oz/225g onion, peeled and
    chopped
  4oz/100g quark
  1 garlic clove, crushed
  1 tablespoon vegetable oil
  ¼ teaspoon paprika
  ¼ teaspoon turmeric
  ½ teaspoon curry powder
  ½ teaspoon ground cumin
  ½ teaspoon ground coriander
  black pepper

Heat the oil and gently fry the onon and garlic for 10 minutes, making sure not to let them brown. Add the paprika, turmeric, curry powder, cumin and coriander and fry for 2 minutes. Remove from the heat and allow to cool. When cool, add the beans and quark, and season with black pepper. Blend until smooth, then transfer to a serving bowl. Cover and refrigerate for a couple of hours.

Cranberry and apple dip

Serves 8

  8oz/225g cooking apple, peeled,
    cored and chopped
  8oz/225g cranberry sauce
  1 tablespoon demerara sugar
  1 dessertspoon light malt vinegar
  1 dessertspoon lemon juice
  pinch of ground cloves

Put the apple, sugar, vinegar, lemon juice and cloves in a saucepan. Cook until pulpy, then allow to cool. Blend the apple with the cranberry sauce until smooth and transfer to a serving bowl. Cover and refrigerate for a couple of hours.

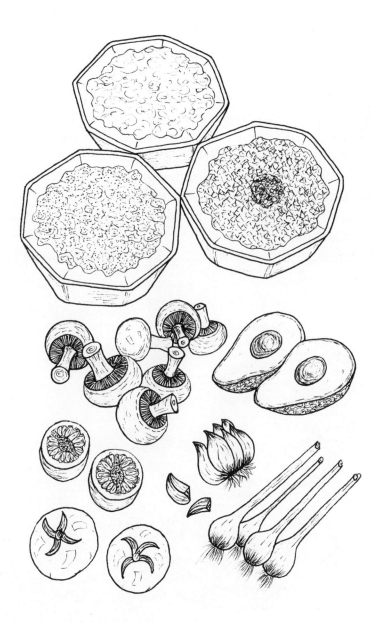

FONDUES

A FONDUE is an ideal dish for serving at informal parties and gatherings. The recipes given here are for making in a traditional fondue pan on the hob of the cooker, then transferring to the buffet table and keeping hot on a fondue burner.

Provide plenty of foods for spearing on long-handled forks for your guests to dip in the fondues. Baskets full of French bread cut into cubes, slices of pitta bread, breadsticks and vegetable crudités all make excellent 'dippers'.

Each fondue is sufficient for about 8 people when served as part of a buffet spread.

Mushroom and Edam fondue

    1lb/450g mushrooms, wiped and
       finely chopped
    4oz/100g Edam cheese, grated
    1 small onion, peeled and finely
       chopped
    1 garlic clove, crushed
    1 tablespoon sunflower oil
    1oz/25g cornflour
    14 fl.oz/400ml milk
    1 tablespoon sherry
    ½ teaspoon yeast extract
    2 teaspoons parsley
    1 teaspoon thyme
    black pepper

Heat the oil and gently fry the onions and garlic for about 10 minutes until soft. Add the mushrooms and cook for another couple of minutes until the juices begin to run.

Dissolve the cornflour in the milk and add to the pan together with the remaining ingredients. Slowly bring to the boil whilst stirring continuously. Continue stirring for a minute or two until the mixture thickens.

Aubergine and Stilton fondue

    12oz/350g aubergine, very finely
       chopped
    6oz/175g blue Stilton, mashed

    4 fl.oz/125ml white wine
    4 fl.oz/125ml water
    10 fl.oz/300ml milk
    1oz/25g cornflour
    2 tablespoons sunflower oil
    2 teaspoons chives
    2 teaspoons chervil
    black pepper
    chopped fresh chives

Heat the oil and gently fry the aubergine for 12–15 minutes until soft. Stir frequently to prevent sticking. Add the wine and water and bring to the boil. Cover and simmer gently for 5 minutes.

Dissolve the cornflour in the milk and add to the pan together with the Stilton and the remaining ingredients. Slowly bring to the boil while stirring continuously. Continue stirring for a minute or two until the mixture thickens. Garnish with chopped fresh chives.

Avocado and Cheddar fondue

    2 large avocado pears
    4oz/100g Cheddar cheese, grated
    4oz/100g quark
    2 tablespoons lemon juice
    1 garlic clove
    1oz/25g cornflour
    5 fl.oz/150ml white wine
    5 fl.oz/150ml milk
    2 rounded teaspoons parsley
    ¼ teaspoon ground bay leaves
    black pepper ➨

57

Peel and chop the avocado pears. Mash them with the lemon juice until smooth, using a potato masher. Cut the garlic clove and rub the inside of the fondue pan with it. Put the wine and grated cheese into the fondue pan: heat gently until the cheese begins to melt, then remove from the heat.

Dissolve the cornflour in the milk and add to the pan together with the mashed avocado and remaining ingredients. Mix thoroughly, then return the pan to the heat. Slowly bring to the boil while stirring continuously. Continue stirring for a minute or two until the mixture thickens.

Cider and apple fondue

  1lb/450g cooking apples, peeled, cored and grated
  8oz/225g Wensleydale cheese, grated
  1 small onion, peeled and finely chopped
  1 tablespoon sunflower oil
  24 fl.oz/725ml cider
  1½oz/40g cornflour
  2 teaspoons Worcester sauce
  ½ teaspoon ground cloves
  black pepper

Heat the oil and gently fry the onion till soft. Add the apple and cook for two minutes. Reserve 4 fl.oz/125ml of cider, and add the rest to the pan together with the

cheese, Worcester sauce and ground cloves. Season with black pepper and bring to the boil. Simmer for a couple of minutes until the cheese melts.

Dissolve the cornflour in the reserved cider. Add to the pan and bring to the boil whilst stirring. Continue stirring for a couple of minutes until the mixture thickens.

Smoky carrot fondue

  1lb/450g carrots, scraped and grated
  6oz/175g smoked Cheddar cheese, grated
  18 fl.oz/550ml water
  4 fl.oz/125ml milk
  1oz/25g cornflour
  1 tablespoon sunflower oil
  1 rounded teaspoon yeast extract
  1 rounded teaspoon chives
  1 teaspoon soy sauce
  black pepper
  chopped fresh chives

Heat the oil and gently fry the carrot for 5 minutes. Add the water. Bring to the boil, cover and simmer for 3 minutes. Transfer to a blender and blend till smooth. Return to the pan and add the grated cheese, yeast extract, teaspoon of chives and soy sauce. Season with black pepper and cook for a couple of minutes until the cheese melts.

Dissolve the cornflour in the milk

and add to the pan. Stir continuously whilst bringing to the boil. Continue stirring until the mixture thickens.

Garnish with chopped fresh chives.

whilst stirring continuously, and continue stirring until the mixture thickens.

Sprinkle the top with grated Parmesan and chopped fresh herbs.

....

Tomato and herb fondue

1lb/450g tin chopped tomatoes, mashed

4oz/100g Cheddar cheese, grated

1 onion, peeled and finely chopped

1 garlic clove, crushed

8 fl.oz/225ml water

2 fl.oz/50ml white wine

1oz/25g cornflour

2 tablespoons tomato purée

1 tablespoon olive oil

1 teaspoon basil

1 teaspoon oregano

1 teaspoon Worcester sauce

pinch of ground bay leaves

black pepper

grated Parmesan cheese

chopped fresh herbs

Heat the oil and gently fry the onion and garlic until soft. Add the tomatoes, grated Cheddar, water, tomato purée, basil, oregano, Worcester sauce and ground bay leaves. Season with black pepper and heat gently until the cheese melts.

Mix the cornflour with the white wine until smooth. Pour into the pan and stir well. Bring to the boil

SAVOURY BISCUITS AND BREADS

AS well as shop-bought savoury biscuits and breads, you might like to serve some home-made varieties. The savoury biscuits and scones given here can all be made the day before and stored in an airtight container. The biscuits look attractive when served in little baskets or bowls either on their own or to go with the Cheese platter (page 21). The scones can be sliced open and served with a savoury filling or paté, or simply spread with butter or margarine.

The savoury breads are best baked about a week in advance and frozen, unless you intend baking them on the day of the party. Thaw at room temperature for a few hours before serving. Even better, then wrap the thawed bread in foil and place in a moderate oven for about 15 minutes to warm before serving.

Sunflower and oatmeal snaps

Makes about 24

4oz/100g medium oatmeal

4oz/100g fine wholemeal self-raising flour

2oz/50g sunflower margarine

½ teaspoon yeast extract

1 rounded tablespoon sunflower spread

3 tablespoons milk

Cream the margarine with the sunflower spread and yeast extract. Work in the oatmeal and flour. Add the milk and mix until the mixture binds together.

Turn out onto a floured board and carefully roll out thinly to approximately ⅕in/5mm thick. Using a biscuit cutter, cut into 2¼in/5½cm circles. Lift the circles on a palette knife and transfer to a greased baking sheet. Re-roll the dough until it is all used up.

Bake in a preheated oven at 180°C/350°F/Gas mark 4 for 10–12 minutes until golden. Transfer to a wire rack and allow to cool.

Cheesy stars

Makes about 20

4oz/100g fine wholemeal self-raising flour

2oz/50g sunflower margarine

2oz/50g Cheddar cheese, grated

1oz/25g medium oatmeal

1 egg, beaten

1 teaspoon mixed herbs

1 teaspoon chives

¼ teaspoon mustard powder

black pepper

milk

sesame seeds

Sift the flour with the mustard powder and black pepper. Rub in the margarine. Stir in the Cheddar, oatmeal, mixed herbs and chives. Add the egg and mix until a soft dough forms.

Turn out onto a floured board and roll out to about ⅕in/5mm thick. Using a star-shaped biscuit cutter, cut out stars. Gather up the remaining pastry and repeat until it is all used up. Transfer the stars to a greased baking sheet, and prick the tops with a fork. Brush with milk and sprinkle with sesame seeds.

Bake in a preheated oven at 180°C/350°F/Gas mark 4 for 10–15 minutes until golden. Transfer to a wire rack and allow to cool.

Peanut oatcakes

Makes 16

3oz/75g medium oatmeal

3oz/75g porridge oats

2oz/50g fine wholemeal self-raising flour ➨

61

2oz/50g sunflower margarine

1 rounded tablespoon crunchy peanut butter

4 tablespoons milk

Put the margarine and peanut butter in a saucepan and heat gently until melted. Remove from the heat and add the remaining ingredients. Mix well until a soft dough forms.

Turn out onto a floured board and shape into an 8in/20cm long sausage shape. Cut into 16 equal slices and shape each slice into a 2½in/6cm diameter circle.

Place the circles on a greased baking sheet and bake in a pre-heated oven at 180°C/350°F/ Gas mark 4 for 15–18 minutes until golden. Transfer to a wire rack and allow to cool.

....

Parmesan and poppy seed crispies

Makes about 30

6oz/175g fine wholemeal self-raising flour

4 tablespoons grated Parmesan cheese

½oz/15g poppy seeds

1 egg

2 fl.oz/50ml sunflower oil

about 2 fl.oz/50ml milk

½ teaspoon paprika

Mix the flour with the Parmesan,

poppy seeds and paprika. Whisk the egg with the sunflower oil until well combined. Make a well in the centre of the dry ingredients and pour in the egg and oil mixture. Mix thoroughly, then add enough milk for the mixture to bind and form a soft dough.

Turn onto a floured board and knead. Roll out thinly and cut into 2in/5cm squares with a biscuit cutter. Carefully lift the squares on a palette knife and transfer them to a greased baking sheet. Re-roll the dough until it is all used up.

Bake in a preheated oven at 180°C/350°F/Gas mark 4 for about 12 minutes until golden. Cool on a wire rack.

....

Sesame and cheese oat fingers

Makes 36

4oz/100g porridge oats

2oz/50g fine wholemeal self-raising flour

2oz/50g sunflower margarine

1oz/25g Cheddar cheese, grated

½oz/15g sesame seeds

1 egg, beaten

1 rounded tablespoon tahini

black pepper

1 teaspoon parsley

Cream the margarine with the tahini in a mixing bowl. Add the egg and beat till smooth. Mix the porridge oats with the flour, cheese, sesame seeds and parsley and season with black pepper. Add this mixture to the mixing bowl and work in until a soft dough forms.

Turn out onto a floured board and knead well. Roll the dough into an oblong shape 12x9in/30x24cm, and cut into 36 3x1in/8x2½cm fingers. Lift the fingers on a palette knife and carefully transfer to a greased baking sheet.

Bake in a preheated oven at 180°C/ 350°F/Gas mark 4 for about 15 minutes until golden. Transfer to a wire rack and allow to cool.

Golden cashew and cheese triangles

Makes 18

2oz/50g crunchy cashew nut butter
2oz/50g sunflower margarine
2oz/50g fine wholemeal self-raising flour
2oz/50g medium oatmeal
1oz/25g wheatgerm
1oz/25g Cheddar cheese, grated
2 tablespoons milk

Cream the cashew nut butter with the margarine. Add the grated cheese and work in the dry ingredients. Add the milk and mix well until a soft dough forms. Turn out onto a floured board and roll out to a 9in/24cm square. Cut this square

into nine 3in/8cm squares, and cut each of these in half to make 18 triangles. Carefully lift them onto a palette knife and lay them on a greased baking sheet.

Bake in a preheated oven at 170°C/325°F/Gas mark 3 for about 10 minutes until golden. Transfer the triangles to a wire rack and allow to cool.

Courgette, cheese and walnut scones

Makes 16

8oz/225g fine wholemeal self-raising flour
4oz/100g courgette, grated
2oz/50g vegetable margarine
2oz/50g Cheddar cheese, grated
1oz/25g walnuts, grated
½ teaspoon thyme
about 3 fl.oz/75ml milk
extra milk
sesame seeds

Rub the margarine into the flour. Stir in the courgette, Cheddar, walnuts and thyme. Gradually add the milk and mix until a soft dough forms. Turn onto a floured board and knead. Roll out to about ⅝in/1½cm thick and cut into 2in/5cm rounds with a pastry cutter. Gather up the remaining dough and re-roll until it is used up.

Arrange the scones on a greased baking sheet and brush the tops with milk. Sprinkle with the sesame seeds and bake in a pre-heated oven at 170°C/325°F/Gas mark 3 for 20-25 minutes until risen and golden. Allow to cool on a wire rack.

Caraway and carrot scones

Makes 14

8oz/225g fine wholemeal self-raising flour

2oz/50g vegetable margarine

2oz/50g carrot, scraped and grated

1 rounded teaspoon caraway seeds

approx. 4 fl.oz/125ml milk

extra milk

poppy seeds

Rub the margarine into the flour. Stir in the carrot and caraway seeds. Gradually add the milk and mix until a soft dough forms. Turn out onto a floured board and knead. Roll out to approximately 5/8in/1½cm thick and cut into 2in/5cm rounds using a pastry cutter. Gather up the remaining dough and re-roll until it is all used up.

Put the scones on a greased baking sheet and brush the tops with milk. Sprinkle with the poppy seeds and bake in a preheated oven at 170°C/325°F/Gas mark 3 for 20–25 minutes until risen and golden. Allow to cool on a wire rack.

Tomato and oregano scones

Makes 12

8oz/225g fine wholemeal self-raising flour

2oz/50g vegetable margarine

2 rounded dessertspoons tomato purée

2 rounded teaspoons oregano

approx. 3 fl.oz/75ml milk

extra milk

onion seeds

Mix the oregano with the flour and rub in the margarine. Mix the tomato purée with a little of the milk until smooth and add this to the mixing bowl. Gradually add the remaining milk and mix until a soft dough forms. Turn out onto a floured board and knead. Roll out to about 5/8in/1½cm thick and cut into 2in/5cm rounds using a pastry cutter. Gather up the remaining dough and re-roll until it is used up.

Lay the scones on a greased baking sheet and brush the tops with milk. Sprinkle with the onion seeds and bake in a preheated oven at 170°C/325°F/Gas mark 3 for 15–20 minutes until risen and golden. Allow to cool on a wire rack.

Peanut scones

Makes 12

8oz/225g fine wholemeal self-raising flour

2oz/50g peanut butter

1oz/25g vegetable margarine

1oz/25g shelled roasted peanuts, finely chopped

approx. 4 fl.oz/125ml milk

extra milk

Rub the peanut butter and margarine into the flour. Stir in two-thirds of the peanuts. Gradually add the milk until a soft dough forms. Turn out onto a floured board and knead. Roll out to about ⅝in/1½cm thick and cut into 2in/5cm rounds using a pastry cutter. Gather up the remaining dough and re-roll until it is all used up.

Arrange the scones on a greased baking sheet and brush the tops with milk. Sprinkle the remaining chopped peanuts on the tops and press in lightly. Bake in a preheated oven at 170°C/325°F/Gas mark 3 for about 20 minutes until risen and golden. Allow to cool on a wire rack.

· ·

Walnut and olive bread

1lb/450g plain wholemeal flour

1 sachet easy-blend yeast

1 teaspoon salt

2oz/50g walnuts

1oz/25g stoned green olives, finely chopped

1oz/25g vegetable margarine

1 tablespoon olive oil

2 fl.oz/50ml warm milk

approx. 10 fl.oz/300ml warm water

extra milk

onion seeds

Put the flour, yeast, salt, walnuts and olives in a mixing bowl and mix. Put the margarine and olive oil in a small saucepan and heat gently until the margarine melts. Add to the mixing bowl, together with the warm milk. Gradually add the water and mix until a soft dough forms. Knead well, then put in the bowl and cover. Leave in a warm place for 30 minutes.

Knead the dough again and shape to fit a greased 7in/18cm diameter deep flan tin. Brush the top with milk and sprinkle with onion seeds. Leave in a warm place for 45 minutes.

Bake in a preheated oven at 190°C/375°F/Gas mark 5 for about 30 minutes until golden and hollow sounding when tapped underneath. Allow to cool on a wire rack. Cut into slices and serve spread with margarine or a savoury spread.

· ·

Sunflower and buck-wheat twist

14oz/400g plain wholemeal flour

2oz/50g buckwheat flour

2oz/50g sunflower seeds

1oz/25g sunflower margarine

1 rounded tablespoon sunflower spread

1 dessertspoon easy-blend yeast

1 teaspoon salt ➔

approx. 12 fl.oz/350ml warm water
milk
extra sunflower seeds

Put the 2 flours, 2oz/50g sunflower seeds, yeast and salt in a mixing bowl. Melt the margarine with the sunflower spread over a low heat, then add to the dry ingredients. Gradually add the water and mix until a soft dough forms. Knead the dough well, then put in the mixing bowl and cover. Leave in a warm place for 30 minutes.

Knead the dough again and divide into halves. Shape each piece into a roll about 13in/33cm long. Twist the two pieces of dough together and squeeze the ends together. Transfer to a greased baking sheet. Brush the top with milk and sprinkle lightly with sunflower seeds. Press these in gently. Cover again and leave to stand in a warm place for 30 minutes.

Bake in a preheated oven at 180°C/350°F/Gas mark 4 for about 25 minutes until golden and hollow sounding when tapped underneath. Allow to cool on a wire rack. To serve, cut into slices and spread with margarine or savoury spread.

Cheese, sage and onion loaf

8oz/225g fine wholemeal self-raising flour
2oz/50g Cheddar cheese, grated
2oz/50g sunflower margarine
1 small onion, peeled and grated
1 egg, beaten
4 tablespoons milk
1 rounded dessertspoon sage
½ teaspoon mustard powder
black pepper
extra milk
sage and onion stuffing mix

Grease an 8in/20cm loaf tin and sprinkle with sage and onion stuffing mix. Shake the tin until all sides are coated with the mix. Sift the flour with the mustard powder and black pepper, and rub in the margarine. Stir in the Cheddar, onion and sage, add the egg and milk, and mix until a soft dough forms. Turn out onto a floured board and knead. Press the dough into the prepared tin and make a slight indent in the top. Brush the top with milk and sprinkle with sage and onion stuffing mix.

Bake in a preheated oven at 180°C/350°F/Gas mark 4 for about 25 minutes until golden. Turn onto a wire rack and allow to cool. To serve, cut into slices and spread thinly with sunflower margarine or a savoury spread.

Parmesan and sesame breadsticks

Makes 16

8oz/225g plain wholemeal flour
2 rounded tablespoons grated Parmesan cheese

1 rounded teaspoon easy-blend
  yeast
1 rounded teaspoon chives
½ teaspoon salt
1 fl.oz/25ml olive oil
approx. 6 fl.oz/175ml warm milk
extra milk
sesame seeds

Put the flour, Parmesan, yeast,
chives and salt in a mixing bowl.
Add the olive oil and warm milk
and mix until a soft dough forms.
Knead well, then return to the
bowl. Cover and leave to stand in a
warm place for 45 minutes.

Knead the dough again and divide
into 16 equal pieces. Roll each
piece of dough into a stick about
9in/23cm long. Brush the sticks
with milk and roll in sesame seeds.
Lay the sticks on a greased baking
sheet and leave to stand in a warm
place for 30 minutes.

Bake in a preheated oven at
190°C/375°F/Gas mark 5 for
about 15 minutes until golden.
Transfer the sticks to a wire rack
and allow to cool.

··

Tomato and garlic rolls

Makes 12

1lb/450g plain wholemeal flour
1 sachet easy-blend yeast
2oz/50g vegetable margarine
2 garlic cloves, crushed
1 rounded tablespoon chives

1 teaspoon salt
2 tablespoons olive oil
2 tablespoons tomato purée
approx. 8 fl.oz/225ml warm water
milk
onion seeds

Put the flour, yeast, garlic, chives
and salt in a mixing bowl. Rub in
the margarine. Dissolve the tomato
purée in the water. Add the olive
oil to the bowl, then gradually add
the tomato water until a soft dough
forms. Knead the dough well, then
return to the bowl. Cover and leave
to stand in a warm place for 45
minutes.

Knead the dough again and divide
into 12 equal portions. Roll each
portion into a ball. Grease an
8in/20cm flan tin and place 9 of
the dough balls round the edge.
Shape the other 3 balls to fit in the
centre. Brush the tops with milk
and sprinkle with onion seeds.
Cover and leave in a warm place
for 30 minutes.

Bake in a preheated oven at 190°C/
375°F/Gas mark 5 for 15–18
minutes until golden and hollow
sounding when tapped underneath.
Allow to cool on a wire rack. Divide
into 12 separate rolls. To serve, slice
each roll open and spread with a
savoury filling or margarine.

SANDWICHES AND SAVOURY SPREADS

DEPENDING on the type of party you are giving, sandwiches can range from dainty little bite-size pinwheels to more substantial filled pitta breads. There is such a huge selection of breads and rolls available from health food shops and supermarkets that no one need ever get bored with the humble sandwich.

Breads and rolls freeze very successfully, so they can be bought in advance and frozen. Thaw them on the day they are needed and fill or prepare near the time of serving.

As well as recipes for sandwich spreads and fillings, this section contains ideas for making your own individual platters.

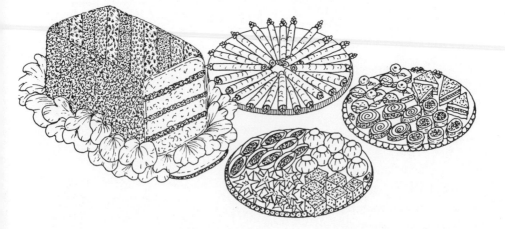

IDEAS FOR SANDWICHES

....

Open sandwiches

Slices of pumpernickel and rye breads are traditionally used as bases for open sandwiches. As well as these, why not try using thin slices of French bread, halved muffins or Granary rolls as bases. Spread the base with a flavoured margarine (page 73) or savoury spread (page 74), then top with a combination of topping ingredients which contrast in colour but complement each other in taste. The following all make ideal toppings for open sandwiches:

Savoury spreads (page 74); spreading patés (page 42); thick dressings (page 92); chutneys and relishes (page 110); slices of cheese, radishes, tomatoes, hardboiled eggs, avocado, apple, apricots, kiwi fruit, peppers and cucumber; shredded lettuce, watercress, spring onions, onion and leek rings, chopped pineapple, halved grapes, olives, chopped nuts, fresh herbs, and gherkins (either sliced or fanned).

....

Pinwheel sandwiches

These little bite-size sandwiches are easy to prepare and prove very popular with children.

Cut the crusts off some medium thickness slices of bread. Roll each slice with a rolling pin to flatten slightly. Spread the slices of bread with a savoury spread right up to the edges. Roll the slices up as you would a Swiss roll, and put the rolls on a plate with the joins underneath. Cover with cling film and refrigerate for an hour. Cut each roll into 6 equal slices. Arrange the slices flat on a serving plate to reveal the pinwheel effect.

For variety, lightly spread the outsides of the rolls with margarine, then roll them in toasted sesame seeds or finely chopped fresh parsley or coriander until coated. Chill and cut as above.

....

Sandwich kebabs

Make up sandwiches using 3 slices of bread with the crusts removed: i.e. use one slice as a base and spread with a savoury spread or paté, put another slice of bread on top and spread with a different savoury spread or paté, and finish with another slice of bread on top. Cut the resulting sandwich into small squares and thread these onto 6in/15cm cocktail sticks, alternating with cherry tomatoes, seedless grapes, olives, slices of celery and cucumber.

For variety, use three different breads sandwiched together.

Nutty stacks

To make 9 little 'stacks' you will need three 4in/10cm square medium thickness slices of bread.

Mix some nut butter with a little fromage frais to make it spread more easily. Spread one slice of bread with the resulting nut spread and place another slice of bread on top. Spread this slice with the nut spread and put the last slice on top. Cut the sandwich into 9 equal squares. Spread the 4 sides of each stack with the nut spread and press these into some finely grated mixed nuts until completely covered.

Sandwich bouchées

Using a 2in/5cm diameter biscuit cutter, cut an even number of circles from some slices of bread. Spread half the circles with a savoury spread or paté. Using a round cocktail cutter, cut a smaller circle from the centre of each of the remaining circles. Place the resulting rings on top of the savoury spread or paté. Pipe or spoon some more spread or paté into the centre hole and top with the bread cut-outs.

For variety, use a 2in/5cm square biscuit cutter to make square bouchées.

Mixed salad and cheese parcels

Cut a wholemeal French stick lengthwise almost all the way through. Spread the inside with a plain or flavoured margarine. Place a layer of shredded lettuce along the whole length of the French stick, followed by some thinly sliced cucumber, finely chopped spring onions, trimmed watercress, and finishing with a layer of grated cheese. Cut the filled French stick into 2in/5cm lengths. Put a cherry tomato or radish onto one end of a cocktail stick and push the other end into one of the parcels to secure. Repeat with all the other parcels and arrange them on a serving platter.

Mini club triangles

Remove the crusts from 3 square slices of medium-sliced bread. Spread one slice with margarine and top with some shredded lettuce. Spread another slice with a savoury spread and put this with the spread side down onto the lettuce. Spread the other side of the bread with the savoury spread and top this with some slices of cucumber. Spread the last slice of bread with margarine and put this with the margarine side down onto the cucumber. Press down lightly, then cut the resulting sandwich with a sharp knife into 4 equal triangles. Cut each of these in half to make 8 mini triangles. Push grapes and small sprigs of fresh parsley onto the ends of cocktail sticks, and stick them in the triangles.

For variety, make toasted club triangles. Toast 3 slices of bread, then remove the crusts. Spread 2 slices with margarine while still warm, then allow to cool before proceeding as above.

Bread baskets

Cut 4in/10cm circles from some medium slices of bread. Push these circles firmly into greased muffin tins. Bake in a preheated oven at 190°C/375°F/Gas mark 5 for about 15 minutes until golden and crisp. Transfer to a wire rack and allow to cool. The baskets can be filled with a savoury spread (page 74), any of the vol-au-vent fillings (page 38), Curried rice salad (page 99), Spanish rice salad (page 99), or anything else that inspires you.

Filled cottages

If you are unable to find tiny cottage rolls, use ordinary tiny rolls and cut a small circle from the top of each with a round cocktail cutter. Gently press the inside of the rolls to make room for the filling. Fill to the top with a savoury spread or a rice salad, and replace the tops to serve.

Mozzarella and chutney griddle rounds

Cut an even number of 2in/5cm rounds from some thick slices of bread using a fluted biscuit cutter. Cut one round of sliced mozzarella cheese for each 2 rounds of bread, using the same cutter. Spread both sides of each circle of bread with margarine. Put a circle of cheese on a round of bread, spread a little chutney over the cheese and top with another circle of bread.

Heat a griddle pan or heavy-based frying pan until hot. Cook the rounds for about 30 seconds each side until golden. Serve warm.

The rounds can be prepared up to the cooking stage several hours before required, and refrigerated.

Burgers and sausages in buns

Use the Pine kernel and mushroom medallions (page 7) as burgers inside little round wholemeal rolls, and the Chestnut and walnut sausages (page 7) for putting inside little wholemeal bridge rolls. Top them both with a chutney or relish to serve.

Asparagus rolls

Cut the crusts off some medium slices of bread. Roll each slice with a rolling pin to flatten slightly. Cook some frozen or fresh asparagus spears until tender, drain, and dry on kitchen paper. Spread the slices of bread with a savoury spread. Trim the asparagus to fit the width of the bread. Put an asparagus spear on one end of a slice of bread and roll the slice up around it. Put the rolls on a plate with the join underneath and cover with cling film. Refrigerate for a couple of hours before serving.

Sesame star toasties

Cut out some small star shapes from thick slices of bread. Toast one side of the stars until golden. Spread the other sides with margarine and sprinkle with sesame seeds. Toast these sides until golden, then tansfer to a wire rack and allow to cool. Pipe a savoury spread in the centre of each star, and garnish.

French bread scoops

Cut a wholemeal French stick into round slices 1in/2½cm thick. Remove a little bread from the centre of each round to make room for a filling. Fill each hollow with a savoury spread, and garnish.

Party sandwich gateau

This savoury gateau makes an impressive centrepiece and can be made as elaborate as you wish.

Remove all the crusts from a large, oblong-shaped wholemeal loaf. Cut the loaf into 4 equal slices length-wise (i.e. the opposite way to which you would normally slice a loaf).

Spread the first slice with a savoury spread and add some finely chopped salad ingredients of your choice. Spread the next slice of bread with a savoury spread, put this with the spread side down onto the salad, and spread the top. Add salad and repeat with the third slice of bread. Finish with a slice of bread that is plain on top. Press the layers down lightly.

Spread a low-fat soft cheese evenly over the sides and top of the gateau. Press the sides in finely chopped nuts until completely covered. Make a pattern of rows, squares or diamond shapes on the top and decorate these with chopped nuts, finely chopped fresh herbs and paprika.

Transfer the gateau to a serving platter and surround with green salad leaves and tomato wedges.

Cut the loaf into 8 equal slices, and each slice into half, to make 16 servings.

FLAVOURED MARGARINES

These are very useful for spreading on savoury biscuits and breads. They're also handy when making sandwiches: they add extra flavour. They are all very easy to prepare, and can be made the day before required.

To make a flavoured margarine, combine the required flavouring with 4oz/100g vegetable margarine, then cover and put in the freezer for an hour or two until firm. Transfer to the refrigerator until ready to use.

If you prefer, you can of course substitute butter for margarine.

To each 4oz/100g margarine, add:

Garlic

3–4 cloves garlic (crushed)

Garlic and herb

3–4 cloves garlic (crushed)

2 rounded tablespoons finely chopped fresh herbs

Lemon and parsley

4 rounded tablespoons finely chopped fresh parsley

2 teaspoons lemon juice

Mixed herb

4 rounded tablespoons finely chopped mixed fresh herbs

Savoury

2 teaspoons yeast extract

1 teaspoon soy sauce

Curried

4 teaspoons mild curry paste

Tomato

4 rounded teaspoons tomato purée

Orange

4 tablespoons finely grated orange peel

2 teaspoons fresh orange juice

Lemon

4 tablespoons finely grated lemon peel

2 teaspoons lemon juice

Mustard

3 teaspoons mustard powder

3 teaspoons water

Mix the mustard with the water until smooth before combining with the margarine.

Minted

2 rounded teaspoons dried mint

2 teaspoons light malt vinegar

Soak the mint in the vinegar for 5 minutes before combining with the margarine.

Piquant

2 teaspoons lemon juice

2 teaspoons celery seeds

1 teaspoon ground bay leaves

a few drops of tabasco sauce

SAVOURY SPREADS

Sunflower and Stilton spread

3oz/75g sunflower seeds, ground
4oz/100g blue Stilton, mashed
1oz/25g sunflower seeds
6 rounded tablespoons fromage frais
4 spring onions, trimmed and finely chopped
2 rounded teaspoons chives
black pepper

Put all the ingredients in a mixing bowl and mix until well combined. Cover and chill until required.

Chick pea, almond and raisin spread

8oz/225g cooked chick peas, grated
2oz/50g ground almonds
2oz/50g raisins, chopped
2 rounded tablespoons almond butter
4 tablespoons milk
black pepper

Put all the ingredients in a mixing bowl and mix until well combined. Cover and chill until required.

Avocado and curd cheese spread

1 large, just ripe avocado
4oz/100g low-fat curd cheese
2 teaspoons lemon juice
1 teaspoon chives
pinch of ground bay leaves
black pepper

Peel the avocado and mash the flesh with the lemon juice until smooth. Add the remaining ingredients and mix thoroughly. Cover and chill for a couple of hours. Avoid making more than 2 hours in advance, to prevent the avocado from discolouring.

Herb and walnut cheese spread

4oz/100g Cheddar cheese, grated
4oz/100g cottage cheese, mashed
2oz/50g walnuts, grated
2oz/50g sunflower margarine
4 tablespoons white wine
½ teaspoon mustard powder
1 rounded tablespoon finely chopped fresh parsley
1 rounded tablespoon finely chopped fresh chives
black pepper

Put all the ingredients into a mixing bowl and mix until well combined. Cover and chill until required.

Carrot, tahini and date spread

8oz/225g carrots, scraped and finely grated

2oz/50g dried dates, finely chopped

4 rounded tablespoons tahini

4 rounded tablespoons fromage frais

1 teaspoon soy sauce

2 tablespoons chopped fresh chives

Put all the ingredients in a mixing bowl and mix until well combined. Cover and chill until required.

Olive and pistachio spread

8oz/225g stoned green olives

2oz/50g shelled pistachios, grated

pinch of ground bay leaves

black pepper

1 rounded teaspoon chives

Blend the olives until smooth. Add the remaining ingredients and mix thoroughly. Cover and chill until required.

Cannellini bean and watercress spread

8oz/225g cooked cannellini beans

1 bunch of watercress, trimmed and chopped

1 tablespoon olive oil

2 teaspoons parsley

2 teaspoons chives

black pepper

Blend all the ingredients until smooth. Transfer to a bowl, cover and chill until needed.

Blue cheese and spinach spread

4oz/100g dolcelatte cheese, finely chopped

4oz/100g frozen cooked chopped spinach, thawed

4 rounded tablespoons fromage frais

1/2 teaspoon marjoram

1/4 teaspoon grated nutmeg

black pepper

Put the spinach in a fine sieve and press out any excess water with the back of a spoon. Transfer the spinach to a mixing bowl, add the dolcelatte and mash together with a fork. Add the remaining ingredients and mix thoroughly. Cover and chill until needed.

Minted bean and cucumber spread

8oz/225g cooked flageolet beans

3oz/75g cucumber, finely chopped

4 spring onions, trimmed and finely chopped

1 tablespoon olive oil

2 teaspoons lemon juice

4 teaspoons dried mint

black pepper

Put all the ingredients except the cucumber into a blender, and blend until smooth. Transfer to a mixing bowl and add the cucumber. Mix well, then cover and chill until required.

Creamy pineapple, raisin and pumpkin seed spread

6 tinned pineapple rings
6oz/175g cottage cheese
2oz/50g raisins
2oz/50g pumpkin seeds, ground
2 spring onions, trimmed and finely chopped
2 teaspoons chervil
black pepper

Pat the pineapple rings dry on kitchen paper, then chop them finely. Add to the remaining ingredients and mix thoroughly. Cover and chill until needed.

Hazelnut and red lentil spread

3oz/175g hazelnuts, ground
3oz/175g red lentils
2 tablespoons sherry
½ teaspoon yeast extract
½ teaspoon Worcester sauce
black pepper

Soak the lentils in water for an hour. Rinse well and place in a fresh pan of water. Bring to the boil, cover and simmer until tender.

Strain the lentils in a fine sieve and press out as much water as possible using the back of a spoon. Transfer the lentils to a mixing bowl and

add the yeast extract and Worcester sauce whilst the lentils are still warm. Stir until the yeast extract dissolves, then cover and refrigerate until cold.

When cold, add the hazelnuts and sherry and season with black pepper. Mix thoroughly. Cover and chill until required.

Curried walnut and lentil spread

3oz/75g walnuts, grated
2oz/50g brown lentils
2 rounded tablespoons low-fat natural set yoghurt
2 rounded teaspoons mild curry paste
1 teaspoon soy sauce
black pepper

Soak the lentils for a couple of hours. Rinse well and put them in a fresh pan of water. Bring to the boil, cover and simmer for about 30 minutes until tender.

Drain in a sieve and press with the back of a spoon to strain all the water off. Mash the lentils with a potato masher, add the curry paste and soy sauce, and season with back pepper. Mix well, then refrigerate until cold.

To retain a crunchy texture, add the walnuts and yoghurt just before serving and mix thoroughly.

Egg, mushroom and parsley spread

2 eggs

3oz/75g mushrooms, wiped and finely chopped

2 rounded tablespoons fromage frais

2 tablespoons finely chopped fresh parsley

1 teaspoon sunflower oil

black pepper

Hard boil the eggs and remove the shells. Chop the eggs and mash with a potato masher. Heat the oil and gently fry the mushrooms for 2 minutes. Add to the mashed eggs, then refrigerate. When cold, add the remaining ingredients and mix thoroughly. Cover and chill until required.

Apple, cheese and sultana spread

8oz/225g red-skinned eating apples, cored and grated

2oz/50g Cheddar cheese, grated

2oz/50g cottage cheese, mashed

2oz/50g sultanas, chopped

2 teaspoons lemon juice

1 rounded teaspoon chives

¼ teaspoon ground cloves

black pepper

Mix the lemon juice and the apple, then add the remaining ingredients. Mix thoroughly, cover and chill until required.

FILLINGS FOR PITTA BREAD

Each filling is enough for 12 picnic-sized pitta breads, or 6 standard sized pitta breads halved. The fillings can be made in advance and chilled for a few hours.

Tomato, mozzarella and mushroom filling

8oz/225g tomatoes

4oz/100g mozzarella cheese

4oz/100g mushrooms, wiped

2oz/50g green pepper

2oz/50g red pepper

2oz/50g cucumber

4 spring onions, trimmed

4 black olives, stoned

1 dessertspoon olive oil

1 tablespoon white wine vinegar

black pepper

1 teaspoon oregano

1 teaspoon parsley

shredded crisp lettuce leaves

Finely chop the tomatoes, cheese, mushrooms, green and red peppers, cucumber, spring onions and olives and place in a mixing bowl. Add the oregano and parsley and season with black pepper. Mix the olive oil with the vinegar and pour over the salad. Toss thoroughly. Put a little shredded lettuce in each pitta bread and fill them with the salad.

Minted mushroom and kiwi filling

12oz/350g button mushrooms, wiped and chopped

3 kiwi fruits, peeled and chopped

6oz/175g tomatoes, chopped

6 cocktail gherkins, finely sliced

3oz/75g quark

1 tablespoon white wine vinegar

3 teaspoons dried mint

black pepper

shredded crisp lettuce leaves

Put the mushrooms, kiwi fruits, tomatoes and gherkins in a mixing bowl. Mix the quark with the vinegar and mint and season with black pepper. Mix until well combined. Spoon over the salad ingredients in the bowl and toss thoroughly. Put a little shredded lettuce in each pitta bread and fill them with the salad.

Apple, celery and walnut filling

3 eating apples, peeled, cored and chopped

3 sticks of celery, trimmed and finely sliced

3oz/75g walnuts, chopped

3oz/75g dried dates, finely chopped

lemon juice

6oz/175g cottage cheese, mashed

3 tablespoons white wine vinegar

1 rounded teaspoon chives

shredded crisp lettuce leaves

Sprinkle the apple with lemon juice and put in a mixing bowl with the celery, walnuts and dates. Mix the cottage cheese with the vinegar and chives and pour over the salad. Mix thoroughly. Put a little shredded lettuce in each pitta bread and fill them with the salad.

Cheese, pineapple and pistachio filling

1lb/450g tin pineapple rings in fruit juice

6oz/175g mixed cheeses (i.e. Gruyère, Edam, Cheddar), diced

6oz/175g ricotta cheese

6oz/175g cucumber, finely chopped

3oz/75g shelled pistachios, chopped

6 cocktail gherkins, sliced

3 sticks of celery, trimmed and finely sliced

2 tablespoons juice from tinned pineapple

2 tablespoons chopped fresh parsley

1 tablespoon chopped fresh chives

black pepper

trimmed watercress leaves

Pat the pineapple rings dry on kitchen paper, then chop finely and put in a mixing bowl. Add the diced cheeses, cucumber, pistachios, gherkins, celery, parsley and chives; season with black pepper. Mix the fruit juice with the ricotta until smooth. Add to the mixing bowl, and mix together thoroughly. Put a little trimmed watercress in each pitta bread and fill them with the salad.

SALADS

BOWLS of colourful and appetising salads are a vital addition to the buffet table. As well as looking very attractive, they are highly nutritious and make a perfect accompaniment for pastries, patés and all other savoury dishes.

Apart from the obvious salad ingredients such as lettuce, cucumber, tomatoes and spring onions, salads can be created by using so many other interesting ingredients. The following recipes also contain a variety of grains, nuts, pulses, pasta, vegetables, cheese and fruit.

Always select the freshest ingredients available and – apart from the Marinated mushrooms, which need to be made the day before – prepare the salads on the day they are required. The bowls of salad can be covered with cling film and refrigerated for a few hours before serving.

Spiced fruit and nut wheat salad

Serves 12

- 8oz/225g bulgar wheat
- 4oz/100g mixed nuts, chopped and toasted
- 4oz/100g dried dates, chopped
- 4oz/100g dried apricots, chopped
- 2oz/50g raisins
- 2oz/50g sultanas
- 20 fl.oz/600ml boiling water
- 8 cardamoms, husked and the seeds separated
- ½ teaspoon chilli powder
- 1 teaspoon ground cinnamon
- 1 teaspoon turmeric
- 1 teaspoon ground coriander
- black pepper
- 4 tomatoes, cut into wedges
- shredded crisp lettuce leaves

Add the bulgar wheat to the boiling water. Cover and leave to stand for 15 minutes. Transfer to a sieve and press out any excess water. Put the drained wheat in a mixing bowl and add the remaining ingredients, except the tomatoes and lettuce. Mix thoroughly.

Arrange the shredded lettuce leaves in a serving bowl. Pile the wheat salad on top and garnish with the tomato wedges.

Cover and chill for a few hours before serving.

Cauliflower, broccoli and tomato salad

Serves 12

- 12oz/350g cauliflower
- 12oz/350g broccoli
- 12oz/350g ripe tomatoes, skinned and finely chopped
- 2 tablespoons white wine vinegar
- 2 dessertspoons olive oil
- 2 teaspoons capers, chopped
- 1 teaspoon fennel seed
- 1 teaspoon basil
- black pepper
- chopped fresh parsley

Cut the cauliflower into small florets. Cut the broccoli stalks into ½in/1cm lengths and the head into small florets. Steam the cauliflower and broccoli until just tender, rinse under cold running water, drain well and put in a mixing bowl.

Mix the chopped tomatoes with the vinegar, oil, fennel seed and basil. Pour over the salad. Add the capers and season with black pepper. Toss thoroughly and transfer to a serving bowl.

Garnish with chopped fresh parsley. Cover and chill before serving.

Chicory, Stilton and Brussels sprouts salad

Serves 12

1lb/450g chicory, finely sliced

8oz/225g blue Stilton, finely chopped

8oz/225g Brussels sprouts

4 sticks of celery, trimmed and finely sliced

2oz/50g walnuts, chopped

16 spring onions, trimmed and finely sliced

16 cocktail gherkins, finely sliced

6 tablespoons white wine vinegar

2 dessertspoons sunflower oil

2 dessertspoons lemon juice

4 teaspoons chives

4 teaspoons chervil

black pepper

chopped fresh parsley

Remove the outer leaves and thick stalks from the sprouts and discard. Finely shred the sprouts and put them in a mixing bowl with the chicory, Stilton, celery, walnuts, onions and gherkins. Add the chives and chervil and season with black pepper.

Mix the oil with the vinegar and lemon juice and pour over the salad. Toss thoroughly and transfer to a serving bowl.

Garnish with chopped fresh parsley. Cover and chill for a couple of hours before serving.

Pepper and tomato salad

Serves 12

2lb/900g mixed peppers (i.e. green, red, yellow, orange)

1½lb/675g tomatoes, skinned and chopped

2 dessertspoons olive oil

4 garlic cloves, chopped

2 tablespoons white wine vinegar

2 dessertspoons tomato purée

black pepper

2 teaspoons parsley

pinch of ground bay leaves

chopped fresh parsley

Put the peppers in a saucepan and cover with water. Bring to the boil, cover and simmer for 5 minutes. Drain and rinse under cold running water, then slice thinly.

Heat the oil and gently fry the garlic until browned, then discard the garlic and add the tomatoes to the pan. Fry the tomatoes until pulpy.

Remove from the heat and stir in the tomato purée, vinegar, dried parsley and ground bay leaves and season with black pepper. Add the sliced peppers and toss well. Transfer to a serving bowl, cover and chill for a few hours.

Garnish with fresh chopped parsley to serve.

Julienne salad

Serves 8

1½lb/675g mixed crisp salad
  ingredients (choose from celery,
  spring onions, carrots, fennel
  bulb, radishes, peppers)
1 bunch of watercress, trimmed
fresh chopped chives

DRESSING
1 tablespoon olive oil
1 tablespoon lemon juice
3 tablespoons white wine vinegar
½ teaspoon dill weed
black pepper

Prepare the crisp salad ingredients,
cut into thin strips about
1in/2½cm long, and put in a
mixing bowl. Mix the dressing
ingredients and pour them over the
salad. Toss well. Arrange the watercress in a shallow serving bowl and
pile the salad on top. Garnish with
chopped fresh chives. Cover and
refrigerate for a couple of hours
before serving.

Carrot, peanut and date salad

Serves 8

1lb/450g carrots, scraped and
  grated
4oz/100g roasted shelled peanuts,
  grated
4oz/100g dried dates, chopped

2 rounded tablespoons peanut
  butter
4 tablespoons water
4 tablespoons light malt vinegar
2 teaspoons chives
1 teaspoon soy sauce
black pepper
shredded crisp lettuce leaves

Mix the peanut butter with the
water, vinegar and soy sauce until
smooth. Put the carrots, dates and
3oz/75g of the grated peanuts in a
mixing bowl, add the chives, and
season with black pepper. Pour the
dressing over the salad and mix
together well. Arrange the
shredded lettuce leaves on a serving
plate. Spoon the salad on top and
sprinkle with the reserved grated
peanuts. Cover and chill for a
couple of hours before serving.

Green lentil and bean salad

Serves 8-10

8oz/225g green lentils
8oz/225g French beans
2oz/50g cucumber, sliced and cut
  into triangles
8oz spring onions, trimmed and
  finely sliced
chopped fresh chives

DRESSING
2 garlic cloves, crushed
2 tablespoons white wine vinegar
1 dessertspoon sunflower oil ➨

2 teaspoons soy sauce
1 rounded teaspoon parsley
black pepper

Soak the lentils for a couple of hours in a large pan of water. Rinse well and put them in a fresh pan of water. Bring to the boil, cover and simmer for about 45 minutes until tender. Drain well and transfer to a mixing bowl. Top and tail the French beans and cut into ¼in/ 5mm lengths. Steam the beans until just tender, then mix with the lentils.

Mix all the dressing ingredients together, and pour over the salad. Cover and chill for a couple of hours. Add the cucumber and onions and mix well. Transfer to a serving bowl and serve garnished with chopped fresh chives.

Curried potato and mushroom salad

Serves 8

2lbs/900g new potatoes, scraped
8oz/225g button mushrooms, wiped and halved
4 rounded tablespoons natural yoghurt
4 tablespoons white wine vinegar
1 tablespoon sunflower oil
2 teaspoons curry powder
2 teaspoons ground coriander
1 teaspoon turmeric
black pepper
2 tablespoons chopped fresh coriander leaves
1 tomato, cut into wedges

Boil the potatoes until tender, drain and allow to cool. Dice them and put in a mixing bowl with the mushrooms. Mix the yoghurt with the vinegar, oil, curry powder, coriander and turmeric and season with black pepper. Mix thoroughly until smooth. Pour over the potatoes and mushrooms and toss well. Transfer to a shallow serving dish and arrange the tomato wedges around the edge. Sprinkle the chopped coriander on top. Cover and chill for a couple of hours before serving.

Minted potato salad

Serves 12

3lbs/1½kg new potatoes, scraped
2 bowls of shredded crisp lettuce
8oz/225g cucumber, sliced and cut into triangles
16 radishes, thinly sliced
8 spring onions, trimmed and sliced

DRESSING

8 tablespoons white wine vinegar
4 dessertspoons sunflower oil
black pepper
4 teaspoons dried mint

Cook the potatoes until tender, then drain and dice. Allow to cool and refrigerate until cold. Transfer to a mixing bowl and add the cucumber, radishes and onions. Mix the dressing ingredients together and pour over the salad.

Toss well, then arrange on top of the lettuce in the bowls to serve.

Marinated mushrooms

Serves 12

  1lb/450g button mushrooms, wiped and sliced
  2 tablespoons olive oil
  4 garlic cloves, crushed
  1 onion, peeled and finely chopped
  black pepper
  4 fl.oz/125ml white wine
  1 rounded dessertspoon parsley
  chopped fresh chives

Heat the oil and gently fry the onion and garlic until soft. Add the mushrooms and fry for 1 minute. Remove from the heat and season with black pepper. Add the white wine and parsley and mix well. Transfer to a serving bowl and cover. Refrigerate for at least 24 hours to allow flavours to be absorbed. Garnish with chopped fresh chives.

Pasta and feta salad

Serves 8

  6oz/175g wholewheat pasta shells
  6oz/175g feta cheese, cut into small cubes
  6oz/175g French beans
  6oz/175g cauliflower
  2oz/50g frozen peas
  2oz/50g frozen sweetcorn kernels
  2 teaspoons marjoram
  black pepper
  1 dessertspoon olive oil
  2 tablespoons white wine vinegar
  chopped fresh chives

Cook the pasta until just tender, then rinse under cold running water and allow to drain. Cut the beans into ½in/1cm lengths and the cauliflower into tiny florets. Steam the beans and the cauliflower until just tender, then allow to cool. Cook the peas and the sweetcorn, drain, and allow to cool.

Put the cooked pasta in a mixing bowl with the beans, cauliflower, peas and sweetcorn. Add the cubed feta and the marjoram and season with black pepper. Mix the oil with the vinegar and pour over the salad. Toss well, then transfer to a serving bowl. Cover and chill for a couple of hours. Serve garnished with chopped fresh chives.

Melon and chick pea salad

Serves 8

  1 small melon (i.e. Charentais, Ogen or Cantaloupe)
  8oz/225g cooked chick peas
  4oz/100g black grapes, halved
  4oz/100g cucumber, chopped
  4oz/100g baby sweetcorn
  2oz/50g button mushrooms, wiped and sliced
  1 teaspoon celery seed ➡

1 teaspoon chervil
curly endive leaves
fresh parsley

Blanch the baby sweetcorn for a couple of minutes, then rinse under cold running water. Drain well and cut into ¼in/5mm rounds. Put in a mixing bowl with the chick peas, grapes, cucumber and mushrooms.

Prepare the melon by removing the seeds and cutting the flesh into balls with a melon baller. Put the balls in a sieve to drain off the juice. Add the melon balls to the salad, together with the celery seed and chervil. Toss well. Arrange some curly endive leaves in a serving bowl. Pile the salad on top of the leaves and garnish with fresh parsley. Cover and chill before serving.

Flageolet bean and vegetable salad

Serves 8–10

1lb/450g cooked flageolet beans
8oz/225g cauliflower, cut into tiny florets
4oz/100g frozen sweetcorn kernels
4oz/100g frozen peas
4oz/100g red pepper, finely chopped
4oz/100g green pepper, finely chopped
2 sticks of celery, trimmed and finely sliced

8 spring onions, trimmed and finely sliced
8 cocktail gherkins, finely sliced
1 tablespoon white wine vinegar
1 dessertspoon lemon juice
1 dessertspoon sunflower oil
black pepper
2 teaspoons parsley
1 teaspoon thyme

Steam the cauliflower florets until just tender. Rinse under cold running water and drain. Cook the frozen sweetcorn and peas, then also rinse and drain. Transfer to a mixing bowl with the cauliflower, flageolet beans, red and green peppers, celery, spring onions, gherkins, parsley and thyme. Season with black pepper. Mix the vinegar with the lemon juice and oil and pour over the salad. Toss thoroughly and transfer to a serving bowl. Cover and chill before serving.

Mangetout, sweetcorn and mushroom salad

Serves 8

8oz/225g mangetout
8oz/225g frozen sweetcorn kernels
4oz/100g button mushrooms, wiped and sliced
8 spring onions, trimmed and sliced
1 dessertspoon sunflower oil
1 tablespoon white wine vinegar
black pepper
1 teaspoon dried mint
2 tomatoes, cut into wedges

Top and tail the mangetout and cut into ½in/1cm lengths. Steam till just tender, then rinse under cold running water.

Cook the sweetcorn until just tender, and rinse likewise.

Put the mangetout, sweetcorn, mushrooms and onions in a mixing bowl and season with black pepper. Mix the sunflower oil with the vinegar and mint and pour over the salad. Toss thoroughly, transfer to a serving bowl, and arrange the tomato wedges around the edge. Cover and chill before serving.

Chicory, carrot and raisin salad

Serves 6–8

3 heads of chicory
8oz/225g carrots, scraped and grated
4oz/100g raisins
1 dessertspoon olive oil
1 dessertspoon lemon juice
2 tablespoons white wine vinegar
2 teaspoons chives
black pepper

Finely slice 2 of the heads of chicory and put in a mixing bowl with the carrot and raisins. Add the chives and season with black pepper. Mix the olive oil with the lemon juice and vinegar, pour over the salad, and toss thoroughly. Separate the leaves from the

remaining head of chicory and arrange in a flower pattern on a serving plate. Pile the salad on top of the chicory leaves. Cover and chill before serving.

Ratatouille

Serves 8–10

1lb/450g courgettes, sliced
8oz/225g tomatoes, skinned and cut into wedges
4oz/100g mushrooms, wiped and sliced
4oz/100g green pepper, sliced
4oz/100g red pepper, sliced
2oz/50g mozzarella cheese, grated
1 onion, peeled and thinly sliced
4 garlic cloves, crushed
1 tablespoon olive oil
2 teaspoons yellow mustard seeds
1 teaspoon mixed herbs
1 teaspoon fennel seed
black pepper

Heat the oil and gently fry the onion and garlic until softened. Remove from the heat and add the rest of the ingredients. Mix well and transfer to a shallow casserole dish.

Cover with foil and bake in a preheated oven at 180°C/350°F/ Gas mark 4 for about 35 minutes until the vegetables are tender. Transfer to a serving dish and serve warm or cold.

87

Oriental salad

Serves 12

1lb/450g tin of pineapple rings in natural juice

8oz/225g Chinese leaves, shredded

8oz/225g beansprouts

4oz/100g red pepper, finely sliced

4oz/100g orange pepper, finely sliced

4oz/100g cucumber, cut into strips

2oz/50g stem ginger, washed, dried and finely chopped

2oz/50g cashew nuts, halved and toasted

2 celery sticks, trimmed and finely sliced

2oz/50g button mushrooms, wiped and sliced

half a small green chilli, deseeded and finely chopped (optional)

DRESSING

2 tablespoons juice from tinned pineapple

2 tablespoons light malt vinegar

1 tablespoon lemon juice

1 dessertspoon sesame or sunflower oil

1 dessertspoon soy sauce

Pat the pineapple rings dry on kitchen paper. Chop them and put them in a mixing bowl with the rest of the salad ingredients, except the cashew nuts. Mix all the dressing ingredients together and pour over the salad. Toss well. Cover and chill for a couple of hours. Add the cashew nuts just before serving and transfer to a serving bowl.

Four grain and vegetable salad

Serves 8–10

2oz/50g long grain brown rice

2oz/50g roasted buckwheat

2oz/50g bulgar wheat

2oz/50g millet

4 fl.oz/125ml boiling water

½ teaspoon yeast extract

4oz/100g leek, trimmed and finely chopped

2oz/50g courgette, finely chopped

2oz/50g carrot, scraped and finely chopped

2oz/50g button mushrooms, wiped and sliced

2oz/50g red pepper, chopped

2oz/50g yellow pepper, chopped

1 celery stick, trimmed and sliced

1oz/25g sunflower seeds

1oz/25g raisins

red and yellow pepper slices

fresh mint leaves

DRESSING

3 tablespoons light malt vinegar

1 dessertspoon sunflower oil

1 dessertspoon soy sauce

1 rounded teaspoon dried mint

1 rounded teaspoon parsley

black pepper

Dissolve the yeast extract in the boiling water. Add the bulgar wheat and leave to stand for 15 minutes.

Put the brown rice, buckwheat and

88

millet in separate pans of water, bring each to the boil and cook until tender. Drain the cooked grains and rinse under cold running water. Drain again and place in a mixing bowl with the soaked bulgar wheat. Add the remaining salad ingredients except the pepper slices and mint leaves.

Mix the dressing ingredients together and pour over the salad. Toss thoroughly and transfer to a serving bowl. Garnish with the pepper slices and fresh mint leaves. Cover and chill before serving.

Beetroot with orange sauce

Serves 8

1½lb/675g freshly cooked beetroot
5 fl.oz/150ml fresh orange juice
3 tablespoons light malt vinegar
1 rounded teaspoon arrowroot
1 teaspoon coriander seeds,
  crushed
¼ teaspoon ground mace
1 orange, cut into wedges

Peel the beetroot and cut into matchstick-size pieces. Put the orange juice and vinegar in a large saucepan, add the arrowroot and stir until dissolved. Add the coriander seeds and ground mace and bring to the boil whilst stirring. Continue stirring until the sauce thickens. Remove from the heat

and add the beetroot. Toss thoroughly until the beetroot is coated with sauce, transfer to a serving dish and cover. Refrigerate for a few hours until cold.

To serve, garnish with the orange wedges.

Tomato and onion salad

Serves 8

1lb/450g tomatoes, thinly sliced
1 bunch of spring onions, trimmed
  and thinly sliced
2 garlic cloves, crushed
1 tablespoon olive oil
3 tablespoons white wine vinegar
1 teaspoon chervil
black pepper
shredded crisp lettuce leaves
chopped fresh parsley

Mix the olive oil with the vinegar, garlic and chervil. Lay the shredded lettuce leaves in a shallow serving bowl. Arrange a layer of tomatoes on top and sprinkle with half the spring onions. Season with black pepper and spoon half the dressing over. Repeat with the remaining ingredients and garnish with chopped fresh parsley. Cover and chill for a couple of hours before serving.

Mung bean and pea salad

Serves 8

4oz/100g mung beans
8oz/225g frozen peas
8 green olives, finely chopped
1 dessertspoon capers
1 heaped tablespoon finely chopped fresh coriander leaves
2 tablespoons white wine vinegar
1 dessertspoon olive oil
1 dessertspoon dried mint
black pepper
2 tomatoes, sliced

Soak the mung beans overnight.

Drain, and put them in a fresh pan of water. Bring to the boil. Cover and simmer for about 40 minutes until tender. Drain well and place them in a mixing bowl.

Cook the peas, then drain and add them to the mung beans together with the olives, capers, coriander and mint. Mix the olive oil with the vinegar and pour over the salad. Season with black pepper and toss well.

Transfer the salad to a shallow serving dish, and arrange the tomato slices round the edge.

Cover and chill before serving.

Borlotti bean and barley salad

Serves 10–12

1lb/450g cooked borlotti beans
8oz/225g pot barley
2oz/50g raisins
4 tablespoons light malt vinegar
1 tablespoon sunflower oil
1 dessertspoon soy sauce
2 teaspoons chives
½ teaspoon celery seeds
black pepper
2 tomatoes, cut into wedges

Soak the pot barley overnight.

Rinse and place in a fresh pan of water. Bring to the boil, cover, and simmer for 30–40 minutes till tender.

Drain and rinse under cold running water. Drain well and place in a mixing bowl with the borlotti beans and raisins.

Mix the vinegar with the sunflower oil, soy sauce, chives, celery seeds and black pepper until smooth. Pour the dressing over the salad and toss well.

Transfer the salad to a serving bowl and arrange the tomato wedges round the edge.

Cover and chill before serving.

Orange coleslaw

Serves 8

12oz/350g white cabbage, finely
  shredded

6oz/175g carrot, scraped and
  grated

2 eating apples, peeled, cored and
  grated

2 small oranges

2oz/50g raisins

1oz/25g walnuts, chopped

4 rounded tablespoons mayonnaise or mayonnaise substitute
  (see page 3)

Put the cabbage, carrot, apple,
raisins and walnuts in a mixing
bowl. Finely grate the peel and
extract the juice from one of the
oranges. Add the grated peel to the
salad. Mix the orange juice with
the mayonnaise until smooth, pour
over the salad and toss well. Put
the salad in a serving bowl.

Now cut the other orange into
slices and use to garnish the salad.
Cover and chill before serving.

Red cabbage and apple coleslaw

Serves 8–10

1lb/450g red cabbage, finely
  shredded

1lb/450g eating apples, peeled,
  cored and grated

4oz/100g sultanas

8 spring onions, trimmed and
  finely sliced

4 rounded tablespoons mayonnaise or mayonnaise substitute
  (see page 3)

4 tablespoons red wine vinegar

lemon juice

black pepper

1 teaspoon black mustard seeds

1 red-skinned eating apple, sliced

Sprinkle the grated apple with
lemon juice and put in a mixing
bowl with the cabbage, spring
onions, sultanas and mustard seeds.
Season with black pepper and mix
together. Mix the mayonnaise with
the vinegar until smooth. Pour over
the salad and toss well.

Transfer the salad to a serving
bowl. Cover and chill for a couple
of hours. Sprinkle the sliced apple
with lemon juice and use to garnish
the coleslaw.

DRESSINGS

IF you want to serve some large bowls of crisp mixed salad
ingredients, you will find a dressing here to enhance and
complement the flavour.

The Green herb and garlic, Orange vinaigrette and Oriental
dressings are all suitable for tossing with the salad ingredients.
Always remember to toss salad leaves in their dressing just before
serving, otherwise they tend to go limp. Also, never add too much
dressing – just enough to cling to the leaves. There's nothing more
unappetising than a bowl of soggy salad!

The other dressings are thicker and are best served in little bowls
with their own separate spoons. As well as for spooning over green
salads, these dressings also go particularly well with rice salads and
ramekins, pastries, patés, and savoury loaves.

With the exception of the Avocado dressing, all the dressings can
be made the day before, covered and kept refrigerated until required.

Green herb and garlic dressing

Makes 7 fl.oz/200ml

2oz/50g fresh mixed herbs
2 garlic cloves, crushed
4 tablespoons olive oil
2 tablespoons white wine vinegar
1 tablespoon lemon juice
black pepper

Remove any thick stalks from the herbs and discard. Roughly chop the herbs. Put them in a liquidiser with the remaining ingredients and liquidise until smooth.

Orange vinaigrette

Makes 6 fl.oz/175ml

4 tablespoons sunflower oil
4 tablespoons fresh orange juice
2 tablespoons white wine vinegar
1 tablespoon finely grated orange peel
black pepper

Whisk or shake all the ingredients together until well blended.

Oriental dressing

Makes 4 fl.oz/125ml

4 tablespoons sesame or sunflower oil
1 tablespoon sherry
1 tablespoon lemon juice
1 tablespoon clear honey
1 dessertspoon light soy sauce
½ teaspoon ground ginger
black pepper

Whisk or shake all the ingredients together until well blended.

Avocado dressing

Makes 9 fl.oz/250ml

1 small avocado pear, peeled and chopped
2 rounded tablespoons fromage frais
2 tablespoons lemon juice
2 tablespoons white wine
1 teaspoon chervil
¼ teaspoon paprika
black pepper

Blend all the ingredients together till smooth. To prevent the dressing from discolouring, avoid making more than 2 hours before serving.

Yoghurt, cucumber and mint dressing

Makes 9 fl.oz/250ml

5oz/150g natural low-fat yoghurt
3oz/75g cucumber
1 rounded teaspoon dried mint
black pepper

Chop the cucumber very finely. Add the cucumber and mint to the yoghurt and season with black pepper. Mix thoroughly.

Mustard dressing

Makes 6 fl.oz/175ml

- 4 rounded tablespoons fromage frais
- 2 dessertspoons water
- 2 dessertspoons white wine vinegar
- 2 teaspoons mustard powder
- black pepper

Mix the mustard with the water and vinegar until smooth. Add the fromage frais and season with black pepper. Mix again until smooth.

Stilton and chervil dressing

Makes 6 fl.oz/175ml

- 2oz/50g blue Stilton, mashed
- 3 rounded tablespoons fromage frais
- 1 rounded tablespoon mayonnaise or mayonnaise substitute (see page 00)
- 1 tablespoon white wine vinegar
- 1 teaspoon chervil
- black pepper

Blend all the ingredients together until smooth.

Peanut dressing

Makes 6 fl.oz/175ml

- 2 tablespoons peanut butter
- 2 rounded tablespoons fromage frais
- 2 fl.oz/50ml boiling water
- 1 dessertspoon lemon juice
- ¼ teaspoon paprika
- black pepper

Mix the peanut butter with the water until smooth. Cover and refrigerate until cold. Add the remaining ingredients and mix thoroughly until smooth.

Creamy garlic and parsley dressing

Makes 9 fl.oz/250ml

- 8oz/225g fromage frais
- 1oz/25g fresh parsley
- 2 garlic cloves, crushed
- black pepper

Remove any thick stalks from the parsley and discard. Chop the parsley finely and combine with the remaining ingredients.

RICE SALADS and INDIVIDUAL RICE TIMBALES

WITH so many different varieties of rice freely available, there are endless possibilities for making some interesting and healthy party dishes.

As well as the various rice salads, rice moulds or individual timbales are easily prepared and can look very impressive.

RICE SALADS

Pineapple and walnut rice salad

Serves 8–10

8oz/225g long grain brown rice

8 tinned pineapple rings, drained and chopped

4oz/100g walnuts, chopped

4oz/100g cucumber, finely chopped

2oz/50g pumpkin seeds

10 spring onions, trimmed and finely sliced

2 tablespoons chopped fresh coriander leaves

2 rounded teaspoons parsley

black pepper

1 tablespoon sunflower oil

2 tablespoons white wine vinegar

fresh parsley sprigs

Cook the rice until tender, then rinse under a cold running tap.

Drain well and put in a mixing bowl. Mix the sunflower oil with the vinegar and pour over the rice. Add the remaining ingredients – except the fresh parsley – and mix thoroughly. Transfer to a serving bowl, cover, and refrigerate for a few hours.

To serve, garnish with the fresh parsley sprigs.

Chick pea, lemon and ginger rice salad

Serves 8

8oz/225g cooked chick peas

6oz/175g long grain white rice

6oz/175g long grain brown rice

2oz/50g stem ginger, washed, dried and finely chopped

1 lemon

6 spring onions, trimmed and finely sliced

black pepper

2 teaspoons yellow mustard seeds

1/2 teaspoon turmeric

1 dessertspoon sunflower oil

Cook the white and the brown rice separately until tender, then drain and rinse both under a cold running tap. Drain well and place in a mixing bowl with the chick peas, ginger, spring onions and mustard seeds.

Wash the lemon thoroughly and cut in half. Cut one of the halves into slices and keep these for garnish. Squeeze the juice from the other half and reserve. Finely grate the peel from the squeezed half and add to the salad.

Mix the sunflower oil and turmeric with the lemon juice. Pour this dressing over the salad and season with black pepper. Mix well, then transfer to a serving bowl, cover, and refrigerate for a few hours. To serve, garnish with the lemon slices.

Black-eye bean and tomato rice salad

Serves 8–10

8oz/225g cooked black-eye beans

8oz/225g firm ripe tomatoes, finely chopped

8oz/225g brown basmati rice

8 spring onions, trimmed and finely sliced

8 cocktail gherkins, finely sliced

1 tablespoon sunflower oil

2 tablespoons light malt vinegar

dash of soy sauce

1 rounded teaspoon dried mint

1 rounded teaspoon thyme

black pepper

2 tomatoes, cut into wedges

fresh mint leaves

Cook the rice till tender, drain, and rinse under cold running water. Drain well and place in a mixing bowl. Add the beans, chopped tomatoes, onions, gherkins, dried mint and thyme and season with black pepper.

Mix the sunflower oil with the vinegar and soy sauce and pour over the salad. Toss well and transfer to a shallow serving bowl. Arrange the tomato wedges around the edge and garnish with the fresh mint leaves.

Cover and refrigerate for a few hours before serving.

Mixed fruit and nut rice salad

Serves 8

8oz/225g brown basmati rice

2oz/50g mixed nuts, chopped

2oz/50g sultanas

2oz/50g raisins

2oz/50g dried dates, chopped

2oz/50g dried apricots, chopped

2oz/50g black grapes, deseeded and quartered

1oz/25g pumpkin seeds

1oz/25g sunflower seeds

1 dessertspoon sunflower oil

1 tablespoon lemon juice

2 tablespoons fresh orange juice

black pepper

1 teaspoon coriander seeds

1 teaspoon parsley

1 teaspoon chives

2 kiwi fruits, peeled and sliced

fresh parsley sprigs

Cook the rice until tender, then drain and rinse under cold running water. Drain well and put in a mixing bowl. Mix the oil with the lemon and orange juices and pour over the rice. Add the remaining ingredients, except the kiwi slices and fresh parsley. Mix well and transfer to a shallow serving dish. Garnish with the kiwi slices and parsley sprigs.

Cover and chill for a few hours before serving.

Curried rice salad

Serves 8–10

8oz/225g brown basmati rice

4oz/100g frozen sweetcorn kernels

4oz/100g red pepper, finely chopped

4oz/100g green pepper, finely chopped

4oz/100g sultanas

2oz/50g flaked almonds, toasted

2 sticks of celery, trimmed and finely chopped

2 eating apples, peeled, cored and finely chopped

8 spring onions, trimmed and finely sliced

lemon juice

DRESSING

4oz/100g fromage frais

3 tablespoons light malt vinegar

3 tablespoons fresh apple juice

2 tablespoons desiccated coconut

1 teaspoon ground cumin

1 teaspoon ground coriander

½ teaspoon turmeric

6 cardamoms, husked and the seeds separated

black pepper

GARNISH

cucumber slices

1 red-skinned eating apple, cored and thinly sliced

lemon juice

Cook the rice until tender, then drain and rinse under cold running water. Drain well and place in a mixing bowl with the red and green peppers, sultanas, celery and spring onions. Cook the sweetcorn, drain, and rinse with cold water. Sprinkle the chopped apple with lemon juice and add to the salad together with the sweetcorn and half the flaked almonds.

Mix all the dressing ingredients together until smooth. Add to the rice salad and mix thoroughly. Transfer the salad to a shallow serving bowl, arrange the cucumber slices round the edge and sprinkle the remaining almonds on top. Cover and refrigerate for a few hours before serving. Sprinkle the apple slices with lemon juice, and use them to garnish the salad.

Spanish rice salad

Serves 8–10

8oz/225g long grain brown rice

8oz/225g tomatoes, chopped

4oz/100g red pepper, finely chopped

4oz/100g green pepper, finely chopped

4oz/100g frozen peas

4oz/100g frozen sweetcorn kernels

2 garlic cloves, crushed

8 spring onions, trimmed and finely sliced

DRESSING

4oz/100g quark

4 tablespoons white wine vinegar

4 tablespoons lemon juice ➜

2 dessertspoons tomato purée
few drops of tabasco sauce
2 teaspoons parsley
1 teaspoon paprika
black pepper

GARNISH
few stoned olives, halved
4 tomatoes, cut into wedges

Cook the rice until tender, then drain and rinse under cold running water. Drain well and place in a mixing bowl with the red and green peppers, garlic, spring onions and chopped tomatoes. Cook the sweetcorn and peas. Drain, rinse with cold water, then add to the bowl.

Mix all the dressing ingredients until smooth, pour over the salad and mix thoroughly. Transfer to a shallow serving dish. Garnish with the olives and tomato wedges. Cover and refrigerate for a few hours before serving.

INDIVIDUAL RICE TIMBALES

Small ramekin dishes, cups, glasses or small bowls are all suitable as moulds for the timbales. Follow your chosen recipe(s), then divide the hot rice into whatever moulds you are using, remembering first to lightly oil the insides of the moulds with sunflower oil. Press the rice down firmly and evenly. Cover with cling film and refrigerate for a few hours or overnight until cold. Run a sharp knife around the edges to loosen, then carefully invert the timbales onto a serving plate. Garnish with the appropriate garnish to serve.

Each recipe makes 8.

••••••••••••••••••••••••••••••

Cheese and tomato timbales

8oz/225g long grain rice
2oz/50g mature or smoked Cheddar cheese, grated
1 onion, peeled and grated
1 tablespoon olive oil
2 rounded tablespoons tomato purée
2 rounded teaspoons chives
black pepper
20 fl.oz/600ml water
2 tomatoes, sliced

Heat the oil and gently fry the onion until softened. Add the rice and fry whilst stirring for 2 minutes. Dissolve the tomato purée in the water and add to the pan together with the chives. Season with black pepper and stir. Bring to the boil, then cover and simmer gently until the liquid has been absorbed and the rice is tender. Remove from the heat and stir in the grated cheese. Spoon the rice into the moulds (see opposite). To serve, garnish each timbale with a tomato slice.

Garlic and parsley timbales

8oz/225g risotto rice
2oz/50g fresh parsley
4 garlic cloves, crushed
1 tablespoon olive oil
18 fl.oz/550ml water
black pepper
8 fresh parsley sprigs

Put the 2oz/50g fresh parsley and the water into a liquidiser and blend until smooth. Heat the oil and gently fry the garlic for 1 minute. Add the rice and fry whilst stirring for 2 minutes. Add the parsley water and season with black pepper. Bring to the boil, then cover and simmer gently until the liquid has been absorbed and the rice is tender. Spoon the rice into the moulds (see opposite). Serve each timbale garnished with a sprig of fresh parsley.

Peanut and raisin timbales

8oz/225g long grain brown rice
2oz/50g raisins, finely chopped
1 onion, peeled and grated
2 rounded dessertspoons peanut butter
1 tablespoon sunflower oil
1 dessertspoon soy sauce
25 fl.oz/750ml water
black pepper
chopped peanuts

Heat the oil and gently fry the onion until softened. Add the rice and fry whilst stirring for 2 minutes. Add the water, raisins, peanut butter and soy sauce. Season with black pepper and stir until the peanut butter dissolves. Bring to the boil, then cover and simmer gently until the liquid has been absorbed and the rice is tender. Spoon the rice into the moulds (see opposite). Garnish each timbale with some chopped peanuts.

Mixed herb and Parmesan timbales

8oz/225g mixed long grain and wild rice
1 onion, peeled and grated
2 garlic cloves, crushed
16 fl.oz/475ml water
4 fl.oz/125ml white wine ➡

101

½ teaspoon yeast extract

2 rounded teaspoons mixed herbs

2 rounded tablespoons grated Parmesan cheese

1 tablespoon olive oil

black pepper

sprigs of fresh herbs

Heat the oil and gently fry the onion and garlic until softened. Add the rice and fry whilst stirring for 2 minutes. Stir in the water, wine, yeast extract and mixed herbs and season with black pepper. Bring to the boil, then cover and simmer gently till the liquid has been absorbed and the rice is tender. Remove from the heat and stir in the Parmesan. Spoon the rice into the moulds (see page 100). Garnish each timbale with a sprig of fresh herbs.

Curried timbales

8oz/225g long grain rice

2oz/50g sultanas, chopped

1 onion, peeled and grated

2 garlic cloves, crushed

1 tablespoon sunflower oil

20 fl.oz/600ml water

1 teaspoon curry powder

½ teaspoon turmeric

½ teaspoon ground coriander

¼ teaspoon cayenne pepper

fresh coriander leaves

Heat the oil and gently fry the onion and garlic until softened.

Add the spices and rice and fry whilst stirring for 2 minutes. Add the water and sultanas and stir well. Bring to the boil, then cover and simmer gently until the liquid has been absorbed and the rice is tender. Spoon the rice into the moulds (see page 100), and serve each timbale garnished with fresh coriander leaves.

Coconut timbales

8oz/225g long grain rice

1oz/25g desiccated coconut

1 tablespoon sunflower oil

1 teaspoon turmeric

½ teaspoon yeast extract

black pepper

20 fl.oz/600ml water

toasted flaked coconut

Heat the oil and gently fry the rice for a few minutes until transparent. Add the remaining ingredients, except the flaked coconut, and stir well. Bring to the boil, then cover and simmer gently until the liquid has been absorbed and the rice is tender. Spoon the rice into moulds (see page 100), and garnish each timbale with a little toasted flaked coconut.

LITTLE NIBBLES AND ACCOMPANIMENTS

IF you've only ever thought of serving bowls of peanuts, crisps and other shop-bought savouries at your parties, read on.

The tasty little nibbles detailed here are all easy to make and look very attractive when served in little bowls or divided serving plates. They are ideal for serving at cheese and wine parties, or as part of a buffet spread.

Also included are recipes for other savoury accompaniments. The three bread-based recipes – Garlic and sesame croûtons, Melba toasts, and Garlic bread – are all old favourites, but nonetheless make perfect accompaniments for other foods in this book. The croûtons go very well with salads or dips, or they can be eaten on their own as a tasty nibble; Melba toasts make suitable 'dippers' for fondues and dips, or they can be served with savoury spreads; whilst Garlic bread is especially good with salads and almost any other savoury dish.

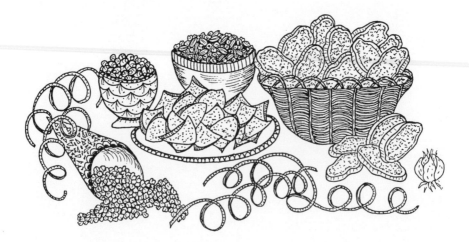

Savoury cocktail puffs

These little puffs can be made the day before you need them and stored in an airtight container.

9oz/250g puff pastry

Cut the pastry into 4 equal portions, then follow the recipes below for each portion. Then bake the puffs in a preheated oven at 170°C/325°F/Gas mark 3 for 10–15 minutes until golden. Transfer to a wire rack and allow to cool.

1 • Peanut pinwheels

Makes 16

¼ of the puff pastry
peanut butter
milk

Roll out the pastry to an oblong shape measuring 9x6in/23x15cm. Spread this thinly with peanut butter, leaving a ½in/1cm border along one of the long edges for joining.

Starting at the other long edge, roll the pastry up tightly like a Swiss roll. Brush the exposed border with milk and press together to join, then brush the roll all over with milk.

Using a sharp knife, slice the roll into 16 equal portions. Lay the slices flat on a greased baking sheet.

2 • Cheese and tomato palmiers

Makes 16

¼ of the puff pastry
½oz/15g Cheddar cheese, grated
tomato purée
½ teaspoon oregano
milk

Roll out the pastry to an oblong shape measuring 9x6in/23x15cm. Spread the pastry thinly with tomato purée, then sprinkle the grated cheese and oregano evenly on top. Roll up both long sides tightly towards the centre. Dampen the edges where they meet with milk, and press together to join. Slice the roll with a sharp knife into 16 equal portions, and lay the slices flat on a greased baking sheet.

3 • Sesame twists

Makes 32

¼ of the puff pastry
sesame seeds
milk

Roll out the pastry to an oblong shape measuring 8x5in/20x13cm. Cut this into 16 ½x5in/1x13cm strips. Cut the strips in half to make 2½/6½cm strips. Dip each piece of pastry in milk, then in sesame seeds, to cover.

Twist each strip like a barley twist and place them on a greased baking sheet.

4 • *Nutty squares*

Makes 40

¼ of the puff pastry

1oz/25g mixed nuts, finely
  chopped

yeast extract

Roll out the pastry to an oblong
shape measuring 8x5in/20x13cm,
and spread thinly with yeast extract.
Sprinkle the nuts evenly on top and
press them down lightly. Cut into
40 1in/2½cm squares, and put
them on a greased baking sheet.

Roasted almonds with sultanas

These can be made a couple of
days in advance and stored in an
airtight container.

8oz/225g blanched split almonds

4oz/100g sultanas

1 tablespoon sunflower oil

2 teaspoons soy sauce

1 teaspoon cayenne pepper

black pepper

Put the oil, soy sauce and cayenne
pepper in a shallow baking dish.
Mix well, then add the almonds
and season with black pepper. Stir
until the almonds are coated with
the oil mixture. Bake in a preheated
oven at 170°C/325°F/Gas mark 3
for about 20 minutes until golden.
Stir once or twice during cooking to
ensure they brown evenly. Remove
from the oven and add the sultanas.

Mix well, and allow to cool before
transferring to a serving bowl.

Celebration mix

2oz/50g shelled peanuts

2oz/50g cashew nuts, halved

2oz/50g Brazil nuts, roughly
  chopped

2oz/50g walnut pieces

2oz/50g hazelnuts, halved

2oz/50g flaked almonds

2oz/50g pistachios

2oz/50g banana chips

2oz/50g raisins

2oz/50g dried dates, chopped

2oz/50g crystallised ginger,
  chopped

1oz/25g pumpkin seeds

1oz/25g sunflower seeds

Mix all the ingredients together
and store in an airtight container
for up to a week before required.
Serve in little bowls.

Savoury popcorn

This popcorn is best made in small
batches. You can make it a day in
advance and store it in an airtight
container.

For each 1oz/25g of popping corn,
you will need:

1 teaspoon sunflower oil

2 tablespoons sunflower oil

1 teaspoon soy sauce

1 teaspoon yeast extract

Heat the teaspoon of oil in a medium-sized saucepan with a lid. Add the popping corn and stir until coated in oil, put the lid on the pan, and heat until all the corn has popped.

Meanwhile, mix the 2 tablespoons of oil with the soy sauce and yeast extract. This will need quite a lot of mixing before it starts to combine.

Remove the popped corn from the heat. Stir the oil mixture again, then pour it evenly over the popcorn. Return to the heat and stir well for about 30 seconds. Allow to cool, then store in an airtight container. Serve in a bowl.

Stilton cocktail bites

Makes about 75

Can all be made a day in advance and stored in an airtight container. Serve in small bowls.

3oz/75g blue Stilton
3oz/75g cottage cheese
2oz/50g ground brown rice
2oz/50g fine wholemeal self-raising flour
1 rounded teaspoon chives
1/4 teaspoon cayenne pepper
milk

Mash the Stilton with the cottage cheese. Add the chives and cayenne pepper, and work in the ground rice and flour. Mix until a soft dough forms. Turn out onto a floured board and knead. Roll to about 1/4in/5mm thick, and cut into tiny shapes with cocktail cutters. Gather up the remaining pastry and re-roll until it is all used up. Transfer the shapes to a greased baking sheet. Brush the tops with milk and bake in a preheated oven at 180°C/350°F/Gas mark 4 for 12–15 minutes until golden. Allow to cool on a wire rack.

Almond and cheese buttons

Makes about 60

Can all be made a day in advance and stored in an airtight container. Serve in small bowls.

2oz/50g ground almonds
2oz/50g fine wholemeal self-raising flour
1 1/2oz/40g sunflower margarine
1oz/25g Cheddar cheese, grated
1/4 teaspoon paprika
1/4 teaspoon mustard powder
milk

Mix the ground almonds, flour, paprika and mustard in a mixing bowl, rub in the margarine, then stir in the grated cheese. Add a little milk to make a soft dough. Turn onto a floured board and roll to 1/4in/5mm thick. With a cocktail cutter, cut into 1in/2 1/2cm circles. Gather up the dough and re-roll until it is all used up. Lay the buttons on a greased baking sheet

107

and bake in a preheated oven at 180°C/350°F/Gas mark 4 for about 15 minutes until they are golden brown. Allow to cool on a wire rack.

Curried peanut balls

Makes about 50

Can all be made a day in advance and stored in an airtight container. Serve in small bowls.

4oz/100g shelled peanuts, ground

2oz/50g fine wholemeal self-raising flour

1oz/25g sunflower margarine

1oz/25g peanut butter

2 tablespoons milk

2 teaspoons mild curry paste

extra milk

Cream the margarine with the peanut butter and curry paste. Add half the ground peanuts, together with the flour and 2 tablespoons of milk. Mix thoroughly until a sticky dough forms. Put the remaining ground peanuts in a bowl. Put a little milk in another bowl. Take half teaspoons of the dough and shape into little balls. Dip each ball in the milk and then in the ground peanuts until completely covered. Transfer them to a lightly greased baking sheet and bake in a pre-heated oven at 170°C/325°F/ Gas mark 3 for about 15 minutes until golden. Cool on a wire rack.

Garlic sesame croûtons

Each slice of bread used makes 20 little croûtons. You can eat them on their own as a tasty nibble, or as an accompaniment to salads or dips. The bread can be prepared up to the toasting stage a few hours in advance, and refrigerated, but the toasting needs to be done just before serving.

slices of square medium-sliced bread

garlic margarine (page 73)

sesame seeds

Spread one side of each slice of bread with Garlic margarine (see page 73). Sprinkle liberally with sesame seeds. Repeat with the other side. Cut each slice into 20 little squares. Toast both sides of the squares until golden under a hot grill. Allow to cool before transferring to a serving bowl.

Melba toasts

Toast both sides of some slices of medium-sliced bread. Trim the crusts from the toasted bread, and cut each slice into 4 triangles. Slice each triangle in half horizontally to make 2 thin triangles. Place them untoasted sides up under a hot grill until crisp. Transfer to a wire rack and allow to cool completely.

Can be made a day in advance and kept airtight.

Garlic bread

Cut a wholemeal French stick into 1in/2½cm diagonal slices. Spread each slice on one side with Garlic margarine (page 73). Wrap in foil and bake in a preheated oven at 190°C/375°F/Gas mark 5 for about 15 minutes. Serve hot.

The bread can be prepared several hours in advance up to the baking stage, and refrigerated.

Garlic and herb bread

Spread the slices of bread with Garlic and herb margarine (page 73). Bake as above.

Garlic and cheese bread

Spread the bread with Garlic margarine (page 73) and sprinkle each slice with a little grated cheese. Bake as above.

Marinated olives

1lb/450g stoned green olives

2 garlic cloves, sliced

2 bay leaves

2 rounded teaspoons coriander seeds, slightly crushed

1 rounded tablespoon grated lemon peel

2 sprigs fresh rosemary

olive oil

Put the olives into a jar or tight-lidded container. Add the garlic, bay leaves, coriander seeds, lemon peel and fresh rosemary sprigs. Pour enough olive oil over the olives to just cover. Put the lid on the jar or container and shake well to distribute the flavourings. Store in a cool place, or in the bottom of the fridge, for at least a week.

Drain the oil from the olives and transfer them to a serving bowl. The oil can be used for cooking or as a base for salad dressings.

Pickled red cabbage

Fills 4 1lb/450g jars

2lb/900g red cabbage

2oz/50g salt

pickling vinegar

4 dessertspoons black mustard seeds

Finely shred the cabbage. Put it in a large bowl, layered with the salt. Cover and leave to stand overnight. Rinse thoroughly, drain, and pack into sterilised jars. Add a dessertspoon of black mustard seeds to each jar. Cover the cabbage completely with pickling vinegar, then seal and label the jars.

Store for at least 10 days before using; jars of pickled cabbage will keep for up to 3 months. Serve in little bowls.

CHUTNEYS AND RELISHES

CHUTNEYS and relishes make ideal accompaniments for salads, patés, pastries, breads and the cheeseboard. Whilst the chutneys given below will store well in a cool, dark place for up to 6 months, the relishes are intended for more immediate use. Store them in the fridge and eat within a few days.

Although chutneys are very easy to make, there are a few important points to remember:

1 Use a heavy-based preserving pan or saucepan, preferably made of stainless steel.
2 Always use a wooden spoon for stirring.
3 Sterilise all jars and lids in boiling water before use.
4 Ensure the lids of the jars used for bottling are vinegar-proof, i.e. plastic or plastic-coated.

To test whether a chutney is cooked sufficiently, draw a spoon through the mixture to expose the bottom of the pan. If the mixture stays separated, and the line you have drawn does not fill with liquid for a few seconds, the chutney is ready for bottling. It will also thicken slightly as it cools.

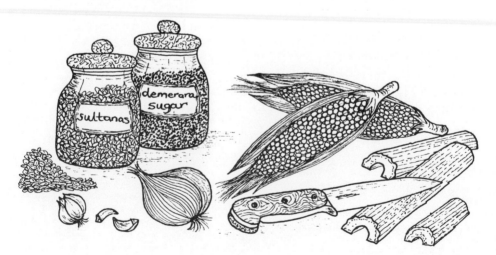

Apple, sultana and ginger chutney

Makes about 4lb / 1¾ kg

3lb/1½kg cooking apples, peeled, cored and finely chopped

12oz/350g sultanas

8oz/225g demerara sugar

4oz/100g stem ginger, finely chopped

12 fl.oz/350ml cider vinegar

2 tablespoons syrup from stem ginger jar

1 tablespoon lemon juice

1 teaspoon allspice

Put all the ingredients in a large saucepan and stir well. Bring to the boil, then simmer uncovered for about 45–50 minutes until the mixture reduces down and thickens. Stir frequently to prevent sticking. Spoon into warm, sterilised jars, cover and label.

Green tomato, apple and mint chutney

Makes about 3lb / 1½ kg

1½lb/675g green tomatoes, finely chopped

1½lb/675g cooking apples, peeled, cored and finely chopped

8oz/225g onions, peeled and finely chopped

8oz/225g demerara sugar

10 fl.oz/300ml light malt vinegar

1 rounded tablespoon dried mint

Follow the instructions for Apple, sultana and ginger chutney.

Banana and date chutney

Makes about 3lb / 1½ kg

1½lb/675g bananas, peeled and sliced

8oz/225g dried dates, chopped

2oz/50g demerara sugar

1oz/50g stem ginger, finely chopped

15 fl.oz/450ml light malt vinegar

¼ teaspoon cayenne pepper

¼ teaspoon ground cinnamon

¼ teaspoon ground allspice

Put the dates, ginger and half the vinegar into a saucepan and bring to the boil. Simmer gently for 3 minutes. Add the remaining ingredients and stir well. Bring back to the boil, then simmer gently, while stirring, for about 10 minutes until the bananas begin to break up and the mixture thickens. Spoon into warm, sterilised jars, cover and label.

Mango and lime chutney

Makes about 3lb / 1½ kg

2lb/900g firm mango, peeled and diced

juice and finely grated peel of 1 lime

6oz/175g onion, peeled and finely chopped ➜

6oz/175g sultanas

2 garlic cloves, crushed

6 fl.oz/175ml light malt vinegar

3oz/75g demerara sugar

black pepper

¼ teaspoon cayenne pepper

¼ teaspoon turmeric

¼ teaspoon ground allspice

½ teaspoon ground mace

1 teaspoon yellow mustard seeds

Put all the ingredients in a large saucepan and stir well. Bring to the boil, then simmer uncovered for about 30–35 minutes until the mixture reduces down and thickens. Stir frequently to prevent sticking. Spoon into warm, sterilised jars, cover and label.

Harvest chutney

Makes about 4lbs/1.75kg

8oz/225g courgettes, chopped

8oz/225g green tomatoes, chopped

8oz/225g red tomatoes, skinned and chopped

2 sweetcorn cobs

4 celery sticks, trimmed and finely sliced

4 garlic cloves, crushed

1 large onion, peeled and finely chopped

2 medium-sized cooking apples, peeled, cored and chopped

6oz/175g demerara sugar

10 fl.oz/300ml white wine vinegar

1 dessertspoon paprika

1 dessertspoon black mustard seeds

1 teaspoon ground mace

¼ teaspoon cayenne pepper

black pepper

Cut the corn from the cobs using a sharp knife and put the kernels in a large saucepan together with the remaining ingredients. Stir well and bring to the boil. Simmer uncovered for about 40–50 minutes until the mixture reduces down and thickens. Stir frequently to prevent sticking. Spoon into warm, sterilised jars, cover and label.

Nectarine and clove chutney

Makes about 3lb/1½kg

2½lb/1.1kg firm nectarines, stoned and finely chopped

6oz/175g demerara sugar

6oz/175g onion, peeled and finely chopped

4oz/100g sultanas

4oz/100g raisins

10 fl.oz/300ml red wine vinegar

1 rounded teaspoon ground cloves

½ teaspoon cayenne pepper

Put all the ingredients in a large saucepan and stir well. Bring to the boil, then simmer uncovered for about 45–50 minutes until the mixture reduces down and thickens. Stir frequently to prevent sticking. Spoon into warm, sterilised jars, cover and label.

Apricot and ginger relish

8oz/225g dried apricots

2oz/50g stem ginger, finely chopped

1 small onion, peeled and grated

4 tablespoons syrup from stem ginger jar

½ teaspoon ground mace

8 fl.oz/225ml white wine vinegar

Soak the apricots in water overnight. Rinse well, drain, and chop finely. Put the apricots in a saucepan with the other ingredients. Stir well and bring to the boil. Simmer gently, stirring frequently to prevent sticking, until the liquid has been absorbed and the mixture thickens. Transfer to a serving bowl. Cover and refrigerate until cold.

Pear, kiwi and lime relish

1lb/450g dessert pears, peeled, cored and finely chopped

3 kiwi fruits, peeled and chopped

juice and finely grated peel of 1 lime

1oz/25g demerara sugar

2 fl.oz/50ml cider vinegar

½ teaspoon black mustard seeds

½ teaspoon chervil

black pepper

Put all the ingredients in a saucepan, stir well and bring to the boil. Simmer gently, stirring frequently to prevent sticking, until the liquid has been absorbed and the mixture thickens. Transfer to a serving bowl. Cover and refrigerate until cold.

Fresh tomato and onion relish

1lb/450g ripe tomatoes, skinned and chopped

8 spring onions, trimmed and finely chopped

4 cocktail gherkins, finely chopped

black pepper

1 dessertspoon olive oil

1 tablespoon white wine vinegar

1 teaspoon parsley

½ teaspoon basil

Mix the olive oil with the vinegar and put in a mixing bowl with the remaining ingredients. Mix together thoroughly, then transfer to a serving bowl. Cover and chill before serving.

Celery, cucumber and apple relish

8oz/225g celery, trimmed and finely chopped

8oz/225g cucumber, chopped

2 red eating apples, cored and chopped

1½oz/40g demerara sugar

5 fl.oz/150ml light malt vinegar ➨

1 teaspoon yellow mustard seeds
black pepper
1 tablespoon light malt vinegar
1 teaspoon arrowroot

Put the celery, sugar, 5 fl.oz/150ml vinegar and mustard seeds in a saucepan and bring to the boil. Simmer for 5 minutes, then add the apple, stir well and simmer for a further 5 minutes. Dissolve the arrowroot in the tablespoonful of vinegar and add to the pan together with the cucumber. Season with black pepper and stir well. Simmer for another 5 minutes whilst stirring. Allow to cool, then refrigerate till cold.

Pineapple and raisin relish

1lb/450g tin pineapple slices in
  natural juice
2oz/50g raisins
1 small onion, peeled and finely
  chopped
1oz/25g demerara sugar
2 fl.oz/50ml white wine vinegar
¼ teaspoon ground allspice
¼ teaspoon ground mace
½ teaspoon ground coriander
black pepper
1 dessertspoon white wine vinegar
½ teaspoon arrowroot

Drain the juice from the pineapple slices. Finely chop the slices and put them in a pan with the raisins,

onion, sugar, 2 fl.oz/50ml vinegar and spices. Stir well and bring to the boil. Simmer uncovered for 10–15 minutes until the liquid has been absorbed and the onion is soft. Dissolve the arrowroot in the dessertspoon of vinegar, add to the pan and stir. Continue cooking for 1 minute whilst stirring. Allow to cool, then refrigerate until cold.

Orange and sultana relish

4 large oranges
4oz/100g sultanas
1oz/25g demerara sugar
2 fl.oz/50ml white wine vinegar
1 teaspoon coriander seeds
½ teaspoon grated nutmeg
½ teaspoon ground ginger
1 teaspoon arrowroot
1 dessertspoon white wine vinegar

Peel the oranges and remove all the pith and membranes. Chop the segments and put them in a saucepan with the sultanas, sugar, 2 fl.oz/50ml vinegar, coriander seeds, nutmeg and ginger. Stir well and bring to the boil. Simmer uncovered for 15 minutes, stirring frequently to prevent sticking. Dissolve the arrowroot in the dessertspoon of vinegar, add to the pan, and stir. Continue cooking for a further minute. Allow to cool, then refrigerate until cold.

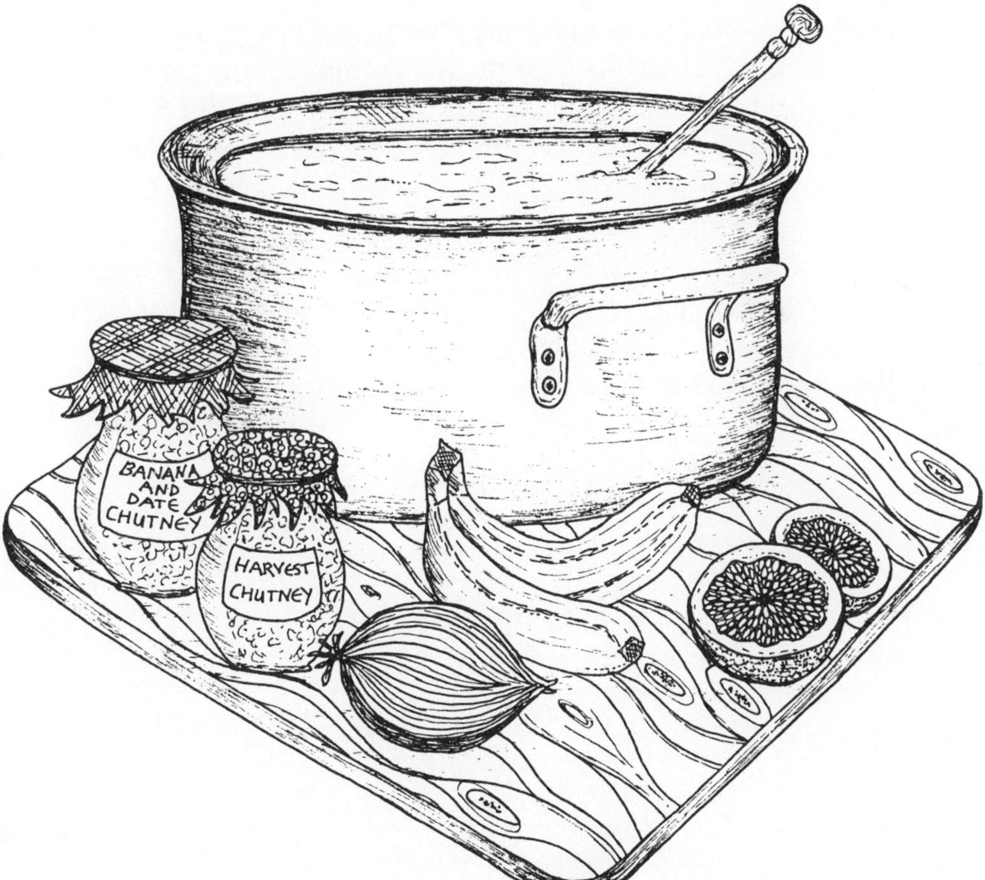
BANANA AND DATE CHUTNEY
HARVEST CHUTNEY

DESSERTS

WHEN it comes to rounding off their meal, you may find that some of your guests will be unable to resist 'sampling' more than one dessert. However, they needn't feel too guilty as none of the desserts featured here is over-laden with fat or sugar.

The Exotic fruit platter with apricot cheese makes a simple yet stunning centrepiece. The apricot cheese can be prepared the day before and refrigerated. The exotic fruits are best prepared a few hours before they are needed, to prevent discolouring of the fruits.

Trifles always prove popular, and the recipe given here for Tropical fruit trifle makes a pleasant change and has a more celebratory feel than the traditional variety. The sponges for the trifle can be made the day before and stored in an airtight tin. The trifle needs to be put together about 6 hours before serving to allow for setting times. Just provide some small bowls, and allow people to help themselves to these two desserts.

The remaining recipes are all for individual desserts which, apart from the Pear, banana and nut crowdies, can all be made the day before and refrigerated until needed. All the recipes can easily be doubled if you wish to make more of a particular dessert.

Exotic fruit platter with apricot cheese

Serves 10–12

3lb/1½kg prepared (i.e. peeled if necessary) exotic fruits: choose a selection from mango, star fruit, paw paw, kiwi, lychee, pineapple, banana, fresh dates and figs, melon, satsumas and grapes.

lemon juice

toasted flaked almonds

toasted flaked coconut

8oz/225g dried apricots

8oz/225g fromage frais

6 fl.oz/175ml fresh orange juice

2 fl.oz/50ml apricot liqueur

First make the apricot cheese. Soak the dried apricots in water overnight. Rinse well and drain, then put them in a saucepan with the fresh orange juice and apricot liqueur. Bring to the boil and simmer gently for about 15 minutes until the apricots are pulpy and the liquid has been absorbed. Stir frequently to prevent sticking. Allow to cool, then refrigerate until cold.

When cold, blend the apricots with the fromage frais until smooth, and put in a serving bowl. Cover, and put it back in the fridge until it is needed.

Now prepare the fruits by cutting them to emphasise their individual shapes. For example, the star fruit, kiwi and banana can be cut into slices. Lychees, dates, figs and grapes can be halved. Satsumas can be segmented, or sliced crossways to make circles, whilst mango, paw paw, pineapple and melon look most attractive when cut into small, even-sized wedges or chunks. Sprinkle any fruits likely to discolour with lemon juice.

Arrange the fruits on a large serving platter with the bowl of apricot cheese in the centre. To serve, scatter the fruit with flaked almonds and coconut.

Tropical fruit trifle

Serves 10–12

SPONGE LAYER

8oz/225g fine wholemeal self-raising flour

4oz/100g vegetable margarine

2oz/50g demerara sugar

2 eggs, beaten

juice and finely grated peel of 2 limes

2 tablespoons milk

ginger jam or marmalade

FRUIT LAYER

1 large, ripe mango, peeled and diced

1 ripe paw paw, peeled and diced

2 passion fruits

JELLY LAYER

20 fl.oz/600ml tropical fruit juice

1 rounded teaspoon agar agar ➔

117

CUSTARD LAYER

30 fl.oz/900ml milk

4 tablespoons custard powder

4 tablespoons dark rum

2 tablespoons demerara sugar

1 teaspoon vanilla essence

GARNISH

1 ripe star fruit, sliced

a few stoned and halved lychees

First make the sponge. Cream the margarine with the sugar, then add the eggs and beat until smooth. Add the flour, juice and grated peel and milk, and mix until smooth. Spoon the mixture evenly into 2 7in/18cm square base-lined and greased sandwich tins. Bake in a preheated oven at 190°C/375°F/ Gas mark 5 for 15–20 minutes until golden and springy when touched. Turn out onto a wire rack and allow to cool.

Spread one of the sponges with the ginger jam or marmalade, and place the other sponge on top. Cut the sponges into small squares and arrange these in the base of a deep, clear bowl of about 10in/25cm diameter.

Mix the mango with the paw paw and the flesh from the passion fruits. Spread the fruit evenly over the sponge.

Dissolve the agar agar in the tropical fruit juice. Put this in a saucepan and heat whilst stirring until just below boiling point. Allow to cool slightly, then pour over the fruit. Cover and refrigerate

for a couple of hours until set.

Put the rum, vanilla essence, sugar, custard powder and a little of the milk in a jug, and mix until smooth. Put the remaining milk in a saucepan and bring to the boil. Remove from the heat and add the mixture from the jug. Stir well and return to the heat. Bring back to the boil whilst stirring. Continue stirring for half a minute until the custard thickens. Allow to cool slightly, then pour over the set jelly. Cover and refrigerate for a few hours until set.

To serve, garnish with the star fruit and lychees.

....

Kiwi and gooseberry cheesecakes

Makes 6

BASES

4oz/100g digestive biscuits, crushed

1oz/25g sunflower margarine

FILLING

8oz/225g quark

8oz/225g gooseberries, topped, tailed and sliced

1oz/25g demerara sugar

2 fl.oz/50ml fresh apple juice

1 teaspoon agar agar

2 kiwi fruits, peeled and sliced

Melt the margarine over a low heat, then stir in the crushed digestives. Mix thoroughly and divide between six 3in/8cm diameter ramekin dishes. Press down firmly and evenly with the back of a spoon.

Put the gooseberries and sugar in a saucepan and cook gently until the gooseberries become thick and pulpy. Mash with the back of a spoon. Allow to cool, then mix with the quark.

Dissolve the agar agar in the apple juice and heat whilst stirring until just below boiling point. Stir into the gooseberry cheese mixture. Beat together thoroughly, then divide the mixture between the six ramekin dishes. Top each dish with kiwi slices, then cover and refrigerate for a few hours until set.

Carob and orange cheesecakes

Makes 6

BASES

4oz/100g digestive biscuits, crushed

1oz/25g sunflower margarine

1 dessertspoon carob powder

FILLING

8oz/225g quark

1oz/25g demerara sugar

1 tablespoon carob powder

5oz/150g orange yoghurt

4 fl.oz/125ml fresh orange juice

2 teaspoons agar agar

1oz/25g orange-flavoured carob bar, grated

1 orange, peeled and sliced

To make the bases, melt the margarine over a low heat, then stir in the crushed digestives and sifted carob powder. Mix thoroughly and divide among six 3in/8cm diameter ramekin dishes. Press down firmly and evenly with the back of a spoon.

Now make the filling. Mix the quark with the sugar, sifted carob powder and yoghurt. Dissolve the agar agar in the orange juice and heat whilst stirring until just below boiling point. Stir into the quark mixture and beat together thoroughly. Spoon the mixture evenly over the biscuit bases and sprinkle the tops with the grated carob. Cover and refrigerate for a few hours until set. To serve, garnish each cheesecake with an orange slice.

Spiced cherry pots

Makes 8

2lb/900g cherries, stoned

2oz/50g demerara sugar

1 tablespoon lemon juice

2 teaspoons agar agar

1 rounded teaspoon cloves

3in/8cm stick of cinnamon, crushed

2 teaspoons allspice berries

8 fl.oz/225ml cherry liqueur

1lb/450g black cherry fruit yoghurt

Tie the cloves, cinnamon and allspice berries in a muslin bag. ➨

119

Reserve 8 cherries for garnish and put the rest in a saucepan together with the sugar, lemon juice and liqueur. Add the muslin bag of spices and stir well. Cover and leave to stand for 1 hour. After standing, heat gently until boiling and simmer for 3 minutes. Strain the liquid into a measuring jug and discard the bag of spices.

Divide the cherries among 8 serving glasses. Make the liquid in the jug up to 24 fl.oz/725ml with water, add the agar agar, and stir until dissolved. Transfer to a saucepan and heat whilst stirring until just below boiling point. Pour the liquid over the cherries in the glasses. Cover and refrigerate for a few hours until set.

Spoon some yoghurt over the jelly in each glass and place one of the reserved cherries on top to serve.

Crunchy raspberry sundaes

Serves 8

  1lb/450g raspberries
  1lb/450g fromage frais
  8oz/225g granola
  4 fl.oz/125ml fresh orange juice
  1oz/25g demerara sugar
  1 rounded teaspoon agar agar

Put half the raspberries in a saucepan with the sugar, and cook gently whilst stirring till pulpy. Pass the pulp through a sieve to remove the pips. Put the sieved raspberries back in the saucepan. Dissolve the agar agar in the orange juice and add to the raspberry purée. Stir well and heat to just below boiling point. Allow to cool, then add the fromage frais and beat until smooth. Divide the mixture between 8 sundae glasses, cover, and refrigerate for a few hours until cold. To serve, top with the granola and the remaining raspberries.

Mandarin mocha desserts

Serves 6

  2 10oz/300g tins mandarin segments in natural juice
  10 fl.oz/300ml milk
  ½oz/15g cornflour
  2 rounded teaspoons decaffeinated coffee powder
  2 rounded teaspoons carob powder
  1 tablespoon demerara sugar
  1 teaspoon vanilla essence
  8oz/225g quark
  10oz/300g mandarin yoghurt
  4 squares orange-flavoured carob block, grated

To make the mocha sauce, dissolve the cornflour, coffee powder, carob powder, sugar and vanilla essence in the milk. Pour into a double boiler and bring to the boil, stirring all the time. Continue stirring until the sauce thickens, remove from the heat, and allow to cool slightly. Add the quark and beat until smooth.

Drain the juice from the tinned mandarins and divide the segments between 6 serving glasses. Spoon the mocha sauce evenly over the mandarins. Cover and chill for a few hours until set. Spoon the yoghurt on top and serve sprinkled with the grated carob.

Pear, banana and nut crowdies

Makes 8

1½lb/675g firm dessert pears, peeled and chopped
1½lb/675g bananas, peeled and chopped
20oz/550g pear or banana yoghurt
2oz/50g ground almonds
2oz/50g medium oatmeal
4 dessertspoons lemon juice
4 dessertspoons maple syrup
2oz/50g cashew nuts, halved and toasted

Put the chopped pear, lemon juice and maple syrup in a large saucepan and cook gently until the pear begins to soften. Remove from the heat, allow to cool, then refrigerate until cold. Mix the ground almonds with the oatmeal and place under a hot grill until golden. Stir a few times to ensure even browning, then allow to cool.

Make up the desserts about an hour before serving. Mix the banana with the pear and divide half the fruit mixture among 8 serving glasses. Spoon half the crumble mixture over the fruit, then a layer of yoghurt. Repeat these layers. Serve with the cashew nuts sprinkled on top.

Mango and ginger cups

Makes 8

2 large ripe mangoes (weighing about 1½lb/675g each)
8oz/225g fromage frais
1oz/25g stem ginger, finely chopped
1oz/25g stem ginger, sliced
4 fl.oz/125ml fresh orange juice
1 rounded teaspoon agar agar

Peel and dice the mangoes. Blend half the diced mango flesh with the fromage frais until smooth. Mix the finely chopped ginger with the remaining diced mango and divide among 8 serving glasses.

Dissolve the agar agar in the orange juice and heat whilst stirring until just below boiling point. Pour onto the blended mango mixture and mix thoroughly. Spoon this mixture evenly over the fruit in the glasses. Arrange the sliced stem ginger on top. Cover and refrigerate for a few hours until set.

121

CAKES

WHATEVER the celebration, the occasion simply wouldn't be complete without a tempting array of cakes. The ones I've included here should satisfy most tastes. There are recipes for small individual cakes, and larger fruit cakes where the fruits have been steeped in alcohol to give them a special celebratory flavour. And there are some easy-to-make tray bakes, useful when serving larger numbers of people.

Also included is a selection of gateau-type cakes (Apricot and almond gateau, Kiwi fruit and coconut sponge, and Hazelnut and mocha sandwich). The sponges for these may be made several weeks before required, and frozen.

Finally, there are recipes for tasty little petit fours, ideal for serving with coffee at the end of your buffet meal. These can look extra special if served in little gold or silver foil petit four cases.

Preparation and storage notes for each cake are given with the recipes.

Carob truffle bowls

Makes 16

These rich little truffle bowls can be made up to 4 days before needed, and are best refrigerated until you are ready to serve them.

BOWLS
8oz/225g carob block

FILLING
8oz/225g fruit cake, finely crumbled
3oz/75g desiccated coconut
2oz/50g sunflower margarine
2oz/50g carob block
2 tablespoons brandy
8 glacé cherries, halved

First, make the bowls. Break the carob block into pieces and melt them in a bowl over a pan of boiling water. Brush the insides of 16 2½in/6cm diameter paper cake cases with the melted carob until completely covered. This is best done in two stages, allowing the first coat to dry slightly before applying the second. Put the coated papers into muffin tins to support the sides, then refrigerate for a few hours until set. Carefully peel the paper cases from the carob bowls and discard.

Next, make the filling. Put the margarine and broken carob block in a saucepan. Heat gently until melted. Add the brandy and stir till smooth, remove from the heat, and stir in the crumbled fruit cake and coconut. Mix thoroughly until well combined. Let it cool slightly, then carefully spoon the filling into the carob bowls. Press the fillings down lightly and place half a glacé cherry on top of each one. Refrigerate for several hours until set. Serve the bowls in foil-covered paper cake cases.

Citrus and ginger buns

Makes 20

Can be made up to 48 hours in advance and stored in an airtight container.

8oz/225g fine wholemeal self-raising flour
8oz/225g cut mixed peel
4oz/100g sunflower margarine
4oz/100g lemon cheese
2 eggs, beaten
4 fl.oz/125ml fresh orange juice
2oz/50g stem ginger

Cream the margarine with the lemon cheese. Add the eggs, and beat until smooth. Stir in the cut mixed peel, flour and orange juice and mix together thoroughly. Put 20 paper cake cases into the holes of a muffin tin and divide the mixture among them. Cut the stem ginger into 20 slices, and put one slice on top of each bun.

Bake in a preheated oven at 180°C/350°F/Gas mark 4 for 20–25 minutes until golden. Leave to cool on a wire rack.

Walnut and cherry yoghurt cakes

Makes 20

Can be made up to 48 hours in advance and stored in an airtight container.

12oz/350g glacé cherries, washed, dried and quartered

8oz/225g fine wholemeal self-raising flour

4oz/100g sunflower margarine

4oz/100g walnuts, grated

2oz/50g demerara sugar

2 eggs, beaten

4oz/100g black cherry yoghurt

TOPPING

3oz/75g icing sugar

few drops of natural red food colouring

a little water

20 walnut halves

Rub the margarine into the flour. Stir in the cherries, grated walnuts and sugar. Add the eggs and yoghurt, and mix thoroughly. Put 20 paper cake cases into the holes of a muffin tin and divide the mixture among them. Bake in a preheated oven at 180°C/350°F/Gas mark 4 for about 20 minutes until golden. Transfer to a wire rack and allow to cool.

Add a little of the red colouring, together with a little water, to the icing sugar, to achieve a pink colour. Mix until you have a stiff spreading mixture. Spread a little of the icing on top of each cake and press a walnut half into it. Let the icing set for an hour or two before serving.

Spicy fruit liqueur cake

Serves 12/16

May be made up to three weeks in advance, wrapped in foil and kept airtight. It needs to be made at least one week in advance, to give it time to mature. Finish with the glacé fruit topping the day before required.

8oz/225g fine wholemeal self-raising flour

4oz/100g sunflower margarine

4oz/100g sultanas

4oz/100g raisins

4oz/100g dried apricots, finely chopped

3oz/75g demerara sugar

2oz/50g dried dates, finely chopped

2oz/50g glacé cherries, washed, dried and quartered

2 eggs, beaten

4 fl.oz/125ml apricot liqueur

1 rounded dessertspoon malt extract

1 rounded teaspoon ground mixed spice

1 teaspoon ground cinnamon

½ teaspoon ground allspice

TO FINISH

2 tablespoons apricot liqueur

2 tablespoons apricot jam
water
a selection of glacé fruits

Put the sultanas, raisins, apricots, dates and cherries in a lidded container. Pour the liqueur over the fruits and stir well. Put the lid on and leave to soak for 24 hours. Stir occasionally.

Cream the margarine with the sugar and malt extract, add the eggs, and beat until smooth. Stir in the soaked fruit, add the sifted flour and spices and mix thoroughly. Spoon the mixture into a lined and greased 8in/20cm diameter loose-bottomed cake tin. Press the mixture down evenly and level the top. Make an indent in the centre, using the back of a spoon, to prevent the cake from rising too much in the middle. Cover with foil and bake in a preheated oven at 170°C/325°F/Gas mark 3 for 50 minutes. Remove the foil and bake for a further 15–20 minutes until a skewer comes out clean when inserted into the middle of the cake.

Leave to cool in the tin for 15 minutes, then turn out onto a wire rack and allow to cool completely. Remove the greaseproof paper, brush the cake all over with the 2 tablespoons of liqueur, wrap in foil, and leave to mature for at least one week before finishing.

To finish the cake, make an apricot glaze by heating the jam with a little water, mixing it until smooth.

Brush the glaze over the top of the cake, then arrange a selection of sliced glacé fruits attractively all over the top. Brush any remaining glaze over the fruits.

Nutty rum and raisin ring

Serves 9

The unfinished ring (that is, before you coat it with the chocolate and hazelnut spread and roll it in nuts) can be made up to three days before you need it, wrapped in foil and kept airtight. It is best finished on the day of serving.

8oz/225g raisins, chopped
4oz/100g fine wholemeal self-raising flour
2oz/50g ground mixed nuts
2oz/50g demerara sugar
4 fl.oz/125ml sunflower oil
2 fl.oz/50ml dark rum
2 eggs
3 tablespoons milk

TO FINISH
1 tablespoon dark rum
chocolate and hazelnut spread
1½oz/40g mixed nuts, grated

Put the chopped raisins in a lidded container, and pour the rum over them. Stir well, put the lid on and leave to soak for 24 hours. Stir occasionally.

Put the eggs, sugar, sunflower oil

125

and milk in a mixing bowl and whisk for a few minutes until they are well combined. Stir in the soaked fruit, ground nuts and flour and mix thoroughly. Spoon the mixture into a greased 8in/20cm diameter sprung ring mould, spread out evenly, and level the top with the back of a spoon. Bake in a preheated oven at 180°C/350°F/ Gas mark 4 for about 40 minutes until a skewer comes out clean when inserted into the cake. If it begins to brown too much, cover the cake with foil for the last 10 minutes.

Pour the tablespoon of rum over the cooked cake and leave it to cool in the tin for 10 minutes. Take it carefully out of the tin and let it cool completely on a wire rack.

Spread the top and sides of the cake lightly with chocolate and hazelnut spread. Roll the outside of the ring in the grated nuts and sprinkle the rest of the nuts on top until it is completely covered.

To serve, cut the ring into 9 equal portions.

Whisky and marmalade loaf

Serves 15

You can make this loaf a week before you need it, wrap it in foil and keep it airtight.

8oz/225g fine wholemeal self-raising flour

8oz/225g cut mixed peel

4oz/100g sunflower margarine

4oz/100g marmalade

4oz/100g dried dates, finely chopped

2oz/50g stem ginger, washed, dried and finely chopped

2oz/50g sultanas

4 fl.oz/125ml whisky

2 eggs, beaten

½ teaspoon ground mace

To FINISH

1 rounded tablespoon marmalade

1 tablespoon whisky

Put the mixed peel, dates, ginger and sultanas in a lidded container. Pour the whisky over the fruits and stir well. Put the lid on and leave to soak for 24 hours. Stir occasionally.

Cream the margarine with the marmalade. Add the eggs, and beat well. Stir in the soaked fruit, add the sifted flour and mace, and mix thoroughly. Grease a 10in/25cm loaf tin and line the base; spoon in the mixture, press it down evenly, and level the top with the back of a spoon.

Cover with foil and bake in a preheated oven at 170°C/325°F/ Gas mark 3 for 1 hour. Remove the foil and bake for a further 10–15 minutes until golden brown, and a skewer comes out clean when inserted into the centre. Leave the cake in the tin.

While the loaf is still hot, sieve the tablespoon of marmalade into a small saucepan. Return the peel to the jar. Gently heat the marmalade in the saucepan until slightly runny, then remove from the heat and stir in the tablespoon of whisky. Prick the top of the hot loaf all over with a thin skewer and brush the marmalade and whisky mixture over the top. Let it cool completely in the tin.

Serve cut into 15 slices.

Malted fig and pecan squares

Serves 18

You can make these the day before and store airtight.

- 8oz/225g fine wholemeal self-raising flour
- 8oz/225g ready-to-eat, no-soak figs, finely chopped
- 4oz/100g pecans, finely chopped
- 4oz/100g sunflower margarine
- 2oz/50g demerara sugar
- 2 rounded tablespoons malt extract
- 2 eggs, beaten
- 4 fl.oz/125ml milk
- 18 pecan halves

Put the malt extract, margarine and sugar in a large saucepan and heat gently until melted. Remove from the heat and let it cool slightly. Add the eggs and beat until smooth. Stir in the figs, chopped pecans, flour and milk and mix well. Spoon the mixture into a lined and greased 14x7in/36x18cm baking tin and level the top. Press the pecan halves gently onto the top so that when you later cut the whole into 18 equal squares, each pecan will be in the middle of a square.

Bake in a preheated oven at 170°C/325°F/Gas mark 3 for about 25 minutes until golden. Turn out onto a wire rack and allow to cool.

To serve, cut through with a sharp knife into the 18 squares.

Banana, Brazil nut and date fingers

Serves 20

You can make these the day before and store airtight.

BASE
- 6oz/175g fine wholemeal self-raising flour
- 2oz/50g sunflower margarine
- milk

FILLING
- 8oz/225g dried dates, finely chopped
- 4 fl.oz/125ml water

TOPPING
- 12oz/350g bananas, peeled and mashed
- 6oz/175g fine wholemeal self-raising flour
- 2oz/50g sunflower margarine ➌

127

2oz/50g demerara sugar

2oz/50g Brazil nuts, finely chopped

3 fl.oz/75ml milk

First make the base. Rub the margarine into the flour, add enough milk to bind, then turn out onto a floured board. Roll out to fit the base of a 14x7in/36x18cm lined and greased baking tin. Prick the base all over with a fork and bake blind in a preheated oven at 180°C/350°F/Gas mark 4 for 5 minutes.

To make the filling, put the dates and water in a saucepan and cook until the dates become soft and pulpy. Remove from the heat and mash with the back of a spoon. Set aside and allow to cool.

For the topping, cream the margarine with the sugar. Add the mashed banana and half the chopped Brazil nuts. Stir in the flour and milk and mix thoroughly.

Spread the date mixture evenly over the pastry base. Spoon the topping over the date mixture and spread out evenly. Sprinkle the remaining chopped Brazil nuts over the top and press them in lightly with the back of a spoon. Return to the oven and bake for about 30 minutes until golden. Turn onto a wire rack to cool.

Serve cut into 20 fingers.

Pineapple, coconut and almond slices

Serves 16

You can make these the day before and store airtight.

1lb/450g tin pineapple rings

8oz/225g dried dates, finely chopped

6oz/175g fine wholemeal self-raising flour

4oz/100g desiccated coconut

4oz/100g ground almonds

4oz/100g sunflower margarine

2oz/50g demerara sugar

2 eggs, beaten

2 tablespoons maple syrup

1oz/25g flaked almonds

Cream the margarine with the sugar and maple syrup. Add the ground almonds and eggs and beat until smooth. Drain the pineapple rings and pat them dry on kitchen paper. Chop the pineapple finely and add to the bowl together with the dates, flour and coconut. Mix thoroughly, then spoon the mixture evenly into a lined and greased 14x7in/36x18cm baking tin. Level the top and sprinkle with the flaked almonds, pressing them in lightly with the back of a spoon.

Bake in a preheated oven at 170°C/325°F/Gas mark 3 for about 30 minutes until golden. Allow to cool slightly in the tin, then transfer to a wire rack to cool completely. Serve cut into 16 slices.

Apricot and almond gateau

Serves 9

You can make the sponges for this several weeks in advance and freeze them. Thaw and assemble with the filling and topping the day before required, and keep in the fridge (it contains soft cheese).

SPONGES

6oz/175g fine wholemeal self-raising flour

4oz/100g sunflower margarine

3oz/75g demerara sugar

2oz/50g ground almonds

2 eggs, beaten

1 teaspoon almond essence

5 fl.oz/150ml milk

FILLING

12oz/350g fresh apricots, stoned and chopped

1 rounded tablespoon demerara sugar

1 tablespoon fresh orange juice

4oz/100g low-fat curd cheese

1 fl.oz/25ml fresh orange juice

1 teaspoon agar agar

TO FINISH

8oz/225g low-fat curd cheese

1 dessertspoon honey

½ teaspoon almond essence

2oz/50g flaked almonds, toasted

4 ripe fresh apricots, stoned and thinly sliced

First prepare the apricots for the filling. Put the apricots, sugar and tablespoon of orange juice in a saucepan and cook until the apricots are pulpy. Stir frequently to prevent sticking. Blend the apricots until smooth, then transfer to a small mixing bowl. Cover and refrigerate until cold.

Next make the sponges. Cream the margarine with the sugar, add the eggs, ground almonds and almond essence, and beat till smooth. Stir in the flour and milk and mix thoroughly. Divide the mixture between 2 base-lined and greased 9in/23cm loaf tins. Spread the mixture out evenly and level the tops. Bake in a preheated oven at 180°C/350°F/ Gas mark 4 for about 15–20 minutes until golden. Turn out onto a wire rack. When completely cool, carefully slice each sponge in half lengthwise to make four 9in/23cm long sponges.

Now finish making the filling. Dissolve the agar agar in the remaining orange juice and heat gently whilst stirring until the mixture thickens. Add to the blended apricots, together with the curd cheese, and mix thoroughly.

Line one of the loaf tins with cling film, and carefully lay one of the half sponges in it. Spread one third of the filling evenly over the sponge. Repeat these layers twice and top with the remaining sponge. Cover and refrigerate for a few hours in the tin until set. ➔

129

Mix the honey and almond essence with the curd cheese until smooth. Carefully remove the cake from the tin and place it on a flat board or piece of cling film. Spread the curd cheese mixture evenly over the top and sides of the cake, then cover completely with the flaked almonds. Arrange the sliced apricots in a row along the top. Carefully transfer the gateau to a serving plate and cut into 9 equal slices.

....

Kiwi fruit and coconut sponge

Serves 10

You can make the sponges for this several weeks in advance and freeze them. Thaw and assemble with the filling and topping the day before required, and keep in the fridge (it contains soft cheese).

SPONGES

6oz/175g fine wholemeal self-raising flour

2oz/50g desiccated coconut

2oz/50g demerara sugar

2 eggs

5 fl.oz/150ml sunflower oil

4 fl.oz/125ml milk

FILLING

4oz/100g low-fat curd cheese

1 rounded teaspoon honey

2 kiwi fruits, peeled and finely chopped

TO FINISH

6oz/175g low-fat curd cheese

1 rounded teaspoon honey

2oz/50g desiccated coconut, toasted

2 kiwi fruits, peeled and thinly sliced

First, make the sponges. Whisk the eggs with the sugar until light and frothy. Add the sunflower oil and milk and whisk again for a few minutes until well combined. Fold in the coconut and flour. Divide the mixture between 2 lined and greased 7in/18cm square baking tins, spread it out evenly, and level the tops. Bake in a preheated oven at 190°C/375°F/Gas mark 5 for 15–20 minutes until golden brown. Turn out to cool on a wire rack.

Next make the filling. Mix the honey with the curd cheese until smooth, then add the chopped kiwi fruits and mix again. Spread the filling evenly over one of the cooled sponges. Place the other sponge on top, and press down lightly.

To finish, mix the honey with the curd cheese until smooth. Spread the sides of the cake evenly with a layer of the curd cheese. Press each side of the coated sponges into the toasted coconut until completely covered. Spread the remaining curd cheese evenly on top of the cake. Sprinkle the remaining coconut over the top and press down lightly. Just before serving, arrange the sliced kiwi fruits in 2 overlapping rows across the top of the cake. Serve cut into 10 equal portions.

Hazelnut mocha sandwich

Serves 8

You can make the sponges for this several weeks in advance and freeze them. Thaw and assemble with the filling and topping the day before required, and keep in the fridge (it contains soft cheese).

SPONGES
- 8oz/225g fine wholemeal self-raising flour
- 3oz/75g demerara sugar
- 1½oz/40g hazelnuts, grated
- 2 eggs
- 6 fl.oz/175ml sunflower oil
- 6 fl.oz/175ml milk
- 1 rounded tablespoon decaffeinated coffee powder
- 1 rounded tablespoon carob powder
- 1 teaspoon vanilla essence

FILLING
- 4oz/100g quark
- 1 dessertspoon demerara sugar
- 1 dessertspoon decaffeinated coffee powder
- 1 dessertspoon carob powder

TOPPING
- 5oz/150g carob block
- ½oz/15g hazelnuts, finely chopped and toasted

Put the sugar, grated hazelnuts, eggs, sunflower oil, milk and vanilla essence in a mixing bowl. Whisk for a few minutes until well combined and smooth. Fold in the sifted flour, coffee powder and carob powder. Divide the mixture between 2 lined and greased 7in/18cm diameter sandwich tins. Spread the mixture out evenly and make an indent in the centre of each to prevent them from rising too much in the middle. Bake in a preheated oven at 180°C/350°F/ Gas mark 4 for about 20 minutes until springy to the touch. Turn out onto a wire rack and allow to cool.

Mix all the filling ingredients together until smooth, then spread evenly over one of the cooled sponges. Place the other sponge on top and press down lightly.

Melt the carob block in a bowl over a pan of boiling water. Spread the carob evenly over the top and sides of the cake, and sprinkle the chopped toasted hazelnuts on top. Refrigerate for a few hours until the carob sets. To serve, cut into 8.

Petit fours

The petit fours in the following recipes can be made up to three days before needed, and stored in an airtight container.

Mocha truffles

Makes about 28

- 3oz/75g fine wholemeal self-raising flour
- 1oz/25g demerara sugar ➲

1 egg

1 tablespoon decaffeinated coffee powder

3 tablespoons milk

1 teaspoon vanilla essence

2oz/50g carob bar, broken

1oz/25g sunflower margarine

2 tablespoons coffee liqueur

chocolate vermicelli

Whisk the egg with the sugar and vanilla essence until light and frothy. Add the sifted flour and coffee powder, together with the milk, and mix well. Spread the mixture evenly into a lined and greased 7in/18cm diameter cake tin.

Bake in a preheated oven at 180°C/350°F/Gas mark 4 for about 15 minutes until golden brown. Turn out onto a wire rack to cool.

Crumble the cool sponge into fine crumbs. Put the broken carob bar and margarine into a saucepan and heat gently until melted. Remove from the heat and stir in the coffee liqueur. Add the cake crumbs and mix thoroughly.

Take heaped teaspoons of the mixture and shape into small balls. Roll each ball in chocolate vermicelli until completely covered. Put the truffles on a plate, cover and refrigerate for a few hours until they are completely set.

Serve in petit four cases.

Peanut and raisin clusters

Makes 32

4oz/100g shelled peanuts, chopped

4oz/100g raisins, chopped

3oz/75g carob block, broken

2 rounded tablespoons peanut butter

Put the carob block and peanut butter in a saucepan and heat gently until melted. Remove from the heat and add the peanuts and raisins. Mix thoroughly, then divide among 32 petit four cases. Cover and refrigerate for a few hours until set.

Marzipan, date and walnut balls

Makes 28

8oz/225g white marzipan

8oz/225g dried dates, finely chopped

1½oz/40g walnuts, finely chopped

Knead the marzipan well, then roll out to an oblong shape measuring 18x6in/46x15cm. Spread the dates evenly over the marzipan. Roll the marzipan up like a Swiss roll to enclose the dates, and cut the resulting roll into 28 portions. Roll each piece into a ball in the palm of your hand, and while the marzipan is still tacky immediately roll each ball in the chopped walnuts. Press the walnuts into the marzipan balls, then transfer to petit four cases to serve.

Lemon and honey cups

Makes 28

- 4oz/100g fine wholemeal self-raising flour
- 2 rounded tablespoons lemon cheese
- 2 rounded tablespoons honey
- 2 tablespoons sunflower oil
- 1 tablespoon lemon juice
- 14 glacé cherries, washed, dried and halved

Put the lemon cheese, honey and sunflower oil in a saucepan and heat gently until melted and well combined. Remove from the heat, stir in the flour and lemon juice, and mix well.

Put a rounded teaspoon of the mixture into each of 28 petit four cases. Press half a glacé cherry on top of each one and bake in a preheated oven at 170°C/325°F/Gas mark 3 for about 12 minutes until golden.

Transfer to a wire rack and allow to cool.

Chewy fig and coffee rolls

Makes 32

- 6oz/175g medium oatmeal
- 4oz/100g no-soak, ready-to-eat figs, finely chopped
- 2 rounded tablespoons malt extract
- 2 tablespoons sunflower oil
- 2 teaspoons decaffeinated coffee powder

Put the malt extract and oil in a saucepan and heat gently until melted, and stir until well combined. Remove from the heat and add the remaining ingredients. Mix thoroughly, then turn out onto a board and knead well. Roll the mixture into a long sausage shape and cut it into 32. Shape each piece into a little roll just over an inch/30mm long. Transfer the rolls to a plate, cover, and keep in the fridge for a few hours until set. Serve in petit four cases.

Coconut and bran balls

Makes about 28

- 3oz/75g d.desiccated coconut, toasted

Put the margarine and carob block in a saucepan and heat gently until melted. Take off the heat and stir in the brandy. Add the 3oz/75g coconut and the bran flakes and mix thoroughly. Take heaped teaspoons of the mixture and shape into balls: this is easier to do if you wet your hands first. Roll the balls in the toasted coconut until completely covered, put on a plate, cover, and refrigerate for a few hours until set.

Serve in petit four cases.

133

DRINKS

AND finally... the drinks. It's easy to overlook the drinks, but when it comes to planning a successful party they're just as important as the food. You can buy in the usual wines, beers, spirits, mixers and minerals, but what better way to welcome people than with a refreshing and appetising *homemade* drink?

All the recipes are easy to prepare, and there's no problem adjusting the quantities to make as much or as little as you need.

Try to position your drinks table away from the food, to minimise congestion. However, there's no need to hide it away; with all the colourful and appealing drinks and garnishes, there's no reason why the drinks table shouldn't look as attractive as the buffet table.

Serve your homemade drinks from large jugs, and have the garnishes already prepared in little bowls, ready to thread onto cocktail sticks. Slice and cut citrus fruit to sit on the rims of some of the glasses. Provide plenty of ice and serve it with tongs from an ice bucket.

It's a good idea to start making ice cubes for your party a couple of weeks in advance. Put the ice cubes in freezer bags as you make them and store them in the bottom of the freezer until you have enough. To make crushed ice, wrap a clean tea towel round a freezer bag containing ice cubes, and tap them with a wooden rolling pin.

Fruit-flavoured ice cubes make a pleasant change and can enhance the right drinks. Make the cubes in the usual way, but use fresh fruit juice instead of water.

ALCOHOLIC DRINKS

Chilled whisky and orange punch

Serves 12

9 fl.oz/250ml whisky

30 fl.oz/900ml dry ginger mixer, chilled

18 fl.oz/550ml fresh orange juice, chilled

15 fl.oz/450ml freshly brewed tea

2 rounded teaspoons coriander seeds, crushed

orange slices

thinly sliced stem ginger

ice cubes

Add the crushed coriander seeds to the hot tea and leave to stand for 30 minutes. Strain and discard the seeds, then refrigerate the tea.

Pour the chilled tea into a punch bowl. Add the whisky, dry ginger mixer and fresh orange juice, and stir well. Float some thin slices of orange on top. Ladle the punch into glasses and add ice cubes. Garnish each glass with half an orange slice and a piece of stem ginger threaded onto a cocktail stick.

Sparkling fruit wine

One 35 fl.oz/1 litre carton of fruit juice and two bottles of sparkling wine will be sufficient to make 14 glasses. For children's drinks, use lemonade or carbonated mineral water in place of the wine, and serve in small tumblers.

For each glass you will need:

2½ fl.oz/65ml fresh fruit juice

4 fl.oz/100ml sparkling white wine

crushed ice

a selection of prepared fresh fruits (to complement the flavour of the fruit juice), threaded onto a cocktail stick

Put some crushed ice in a wine or champagne glass. Pour the fruit juice over the ice, then add sparkling wine. Serve with the fruit-threaded cocktail stick resting on the rim of the glass.

Exotic fruit cocktail

Serves 12

2 14oz/400g tins of exotic fruit cocktail in natural juice

24 fl.oz/725ml soda water

20 fl.oz/600ml tropical fruit juice

12 fl.oz/350ml fruit liqueur

ice cubes

cubed pineapple

Put the contents of the 2 tins of

fruit (i.e. both fruit and juice) into a liquidiser, add the tropical fruit juice, and liquidise until smooth. Pour the liquid through a fine sieve, then add the soda water and liqueur. Stir very well, then chill.

Stir the drink again before pouring into small tumblers. Add some ice cubes, and garnish each glass with cubed pineapple threaded onto a cocktail stick.

Cider and ginger cooler

Serves 12

40 fl.oz/1200ml dry cider, chilled

40 fl.oz/1200ml dry ginger mixer, chilled

40 fl.oz/1200ml fresh apple juice, chilled

2 fl.oz/50ml brandy

ice cubes

chopped stem ginger

1 red-skinned eating apple, cored and sliced

Mix the cider with the dry ginger mixer, apple juice and brandy. Pour over ice cubes in long tumblers. Float an apple slice in each tumbler and garnish each drink with a piece of stem ginger threaded onto a cocktail stick.

Cherry velvet

Serves 12

1lb/450g black cherry yoghurt

8 fl.oz/225ml cherry brandy

40 fl.oz/1200ml soda water

cocktail cherries

Liquidise the yoghurt, cherry brandy and soda water until smooth. Refrigerate until cold, then stir well before pouring into wine glasses. Garnish each glass with a cocktail cherry on a stick.

Minted kiwi refresher

Serves 8

2 ripe kiwi fruits, peeled and chopped

10 fl.oz/300ml dry vermouth

28 fl.oz/825ml tonic water, chilled

1 rounded dessertspoon chopped fresh mint

kiwi slices

fresh mint leaves

ice cubes

Liquidise the chopped kiwis, dry vermouth and chopped mint until smooth. Pass through a fine sieve, then refrigerate. Add the tonic water and stir well. Pour over ice cubes in wine glasses. Sit a kiwi slice on the rim of each glass and garnish with fresh mint leaves.

Strawberry blush

Serves 12

- 12oz/350g ripe strawberries, chopped
- 12 fl.oz/350ml sweet vermouth
- 48 fl.oz/1425ml sparkling rosé wine, chilled
- whole strawberries
- crushed ice

Liquidise the chopped strawberries with the vermouth until smooth. Pass through a fine sieve, then refrigerate until cold. Add the wine and stir well. Pour over crushed ice in wine glasses. Thread strawberries onto cocktail sticks to garnish the glasses as you serve them.

NON-ALCOHOLIC DRINKS

Apple, sultana and honey tonic

Serves 12

- 1lb/450g cooking apples, peeled, cored and chopped
- 2oz/50g sultanas
- 2 teaspoons lemon juice
- 2 dessertspoons clear honey
- 4 tablespoons water
- 48 fl.oz/1425ml tonic water, chilled
- crushed ice
- 1 large red-skinned eating apple
- extra lemon juice

Put the chopped cooking apple, sultanas, honey, water and 2 teaspoons of lemon juice in a saucepan. Cook gently until the apple becomes soft and pulpy. Put in a covered bowl in the fridge.

When cold, liquidise the cooked apple mixture with the tonic water until smooth. Strain through a fine sieve, and pour it over crushed ice in small tumblers. Remove the core from the red-skinned apple and discard. Cut the apple into 12 slices and sprinkle each slice with lemon juice. Serve each glass topped with an apple slice.

Banana and maple ripple

Serves 12

12oz/350g bananas, peeled and chopped

7oz/200g banana fromage frais

3 tablespoons maple syrup

24 fl.oz/725ml sparkling mineral water

24 fl.oz/725ml soda water

ice cubes

banana slices

lemon juice

Liquidise the chopped banana, fromage frais, maple syrup and mineral water until smooth. Refrigerate until cold, then add the soda water and stir well. Pour over ice cubes in wine glasses. Sprinkle the banana slices with lemon juice, thread them onto cocktail sticks, and use to garnish each glass.

Barley and citrus quencher

Serves 12

4oz/100g pot barley

80 fl.oz/2400ml litres water

20 fl.oz/600ml fresh orange juice, chilled

2 large lemons

4 rounded dessertspoons clear honey

crushed ice

orange slices

lemon peel twists

Wash the pot barley and put it in a large saucepan with the water. Wash the lemons thoroughly, extract the juice and add it to the pan. Remove the pith and membranes from the sqeezed lemons and discard: chop the peel and add to the pan. Bring to the boil, cover, and simmer briskly for 30 minutes.

Strain the liquid into a large jug or bowl. Add the honey to the hot liquid and stir until dissolved. Cover and allow to cool, then refrigerate until cold. Add the chilled orange juice and stir well. Pour over crushed ice in long tumblers. Garnish with an orange slice and a twist of lemon peel.

Iced mocha cream

Serves 12

60 fl.oz/1800ml boiling water

3 rounded tablespoons decaffeinated coffee granules

1 teaspoon vanilla essence

4oz/100g carob bar, broken

6oz/175g vanilla ice cream

grated carob

Melt the broken carob bar in a bowl over a pan of boiling water. Dissolve the coffee granules and vanilla essence in the boiling water, then add the melted carob and stir well. Cover and leave to cool, then refrigerate overnight.

Just before serving, add the ice cream and liquidise until smooth.

Pour into small tumblers and serve sprinkled with grated carob.

Grapefruit and apple sparkle

Serves 12

> 3 1lb 3oz/525g tins of grapefruit in natural juice
>
> 54 fl.oz/1600ml sparkling apple juice, chilled
>
> ice cubes
>
> thin grapefruit slices
>
> black seedless grapes

Liquidise the contents of the tins of grapefruit (fruit and juice) until smooth. Add the sparkling apple juice and pass through a fine sieve. Pour over ice cubes in long tumblers. Spear a grapefruit twist and a couple of black grapes onto a cocktail stick and use one to garnish each glass.

Tomato and cucumber cocktail

Serves 8

> 30 fl.oz/900ml tomato juice
>
> 8oz/225g cucumber, chopped
>
> 8 fl.oz/225ml mineral water
>
> 1 teaspoon lemon juice
>
> 1 teaspoon Worcester sauce
>
> 1 teaspoon soy sauce
>
> cucumber slices
>
> fresh mint leaves

Put the tomato juice, chopped cucumber, mineral water, lemon juice, Worcester sauce and soy sauce in a liquidiser and liquidise until smooth. Pass through a fine sieve and refrigerate until cold. Pour into wine glasses and garnish each with a cucumber twist threaded onto a cocktail stick and fresh mint leaves.

Melon and grape surprise

Serves 10

> 1lb/450g ripe honeydew melon, peeled and chopped
>
> 40 fl.oz/1200ml white grape juice
>
> melon balls
>
> black and green seedless grapes

Liquidise the chopped melon with the grape juice until smooth, then refrigerate until cold. Make 30 small melon balls with a melon ball cutter. Spread the melon balls out in a freezer-proof container, making sure they do not touch one another, and freeze them for a couple of hours till frozen.

Stir the drink and pour it into small tumblers. Add 3 iced melon balls to each glass, and garnish with black and green grapes threaded onto cocktail sticks.

Recipes and notes

Recipes and notes

Recipes and notes

Recipes and notes

Recipes and notes

146

Recipes and notes

Recipes and notes

Other books from Jon Carpenter

Vegetarian Visitor
Edited by ANNEMARIE WEITZEL
An annual guide to vegetarian accommodation in Britain

Living Without Cruelty Diary
Edited by MARK GOLD
‣Features, photographs and recipes for vegetarians,
animal campaigners and greens everywhere.
Includes a Directory of green organisations.
New edition each year

Beyond Optimism
KEN JONES
The importance of combining social activism with 'inner work'.
A major work of cultural analysis from a Buddhist perspective
1 897766 06 8   £9.99

Caught in the Act: The Feldberg Investigation
MELODY MACDONALD
How animal campaigners infiltrated the laboratory of a
vivisector and revealed his malpractices to the media
1 897766 05 X   £4.99

Days of Decision
DAVID ICKE
A remarkable combination of political insight and spiritual
wisdom. A new creation story for our times
1 897766 01 7   £5.99

Jon Carpenter books are available from good bookshops,
or by post from
JON CARPENTER PUBLISHING, PO BOX 129, OXFORD OX1 4PH